Overcoming Insecure Attachment

Overcoming Insecure Attachment

8 Proven Steps to Recognizing Anxious and Avoidant Attachment Styles and Building Healthier, Happier Relationships

TRACY CROSSLEY, MA

 ULYSSES PRESS

Published in the US by:
ULYSSES PRESS
PO Box 3440
Berkeley, CA 94703
www.ulyssespress.com

ISBN: 978-1-64604-250-0
Library of Congress Control Number: 2021937752

Printed in the United States by Kingery Printing Company
10 9 8 7 6 5 4 3 2 1

Acquisitions editor: Claire Sielaff
Managing editor: Claire Chun
Editor: Renee Rutledge
Proofreader: Barbara Schultz
Front cover design: Christopher Cote
Cover artwork: © Andrew Krasovitckii/shutterstock.com
Interior design: what!design @ whatweb.com
Production: Jake Flaherty

To my husband, David—my rock, my greatest support, and my love!

Contents

CHAPTER 9

Step 6—Stop Assuming and Personalizing 181

CHAPTER 10

Step 7—Start Taking Responsibility 203

CHAPTER 11

Step 8—Start Feeling Your Real Feelings 225

Preface

I wish I had this book back when I was struggling. I was in so much emotional pain because of how I chose to live my life. I was a perfectionist, a people pleaser, and an emotional avoidant who had an anxiety problem. On top of this, I spent a ton of time solving everyone else's problems while pretending I had none of my own. I was an expert at hiding my pain.

No one really knew how much I suffered. Even if someone had an inkling, I would make sure they understood it was a temporary setback which I was resolving quickly. I could not handle anyone feeling sorry for me or giving me unwanted advice. I thought I knew it all.

Being a perfectionist and a problem-solver meant I could never rest on my laurels. I was always doing and striving to get validation from my accomplishments. When I did not get that validation, I punished myself. Somehow, I needed to suffer when I was rejected, disappointed, made mistakes, or did something else that could possibly put a chink in how I was perceived by the rest of the world.

I don't want to leave you alone on the same road, driving around in circles looking for the turnoff to happiness. That's why I wrote this book.

MY JOURNEY TO EMOTIONAL FREEDOM

I am a behavioral relationship expert trained in a form of ontological coaching, which brings together body, mind, and soul. This style of coaching leads individuals to more self-awareness based on their way of being; it addresses issues from an emotional, somatic, and spiritual perspective.

My work has centered on emotional connection—with ourselves and with others. I have helped thousands of people get out of their thinking minds and take emotionally driven actions that break the patterns that keep them stuck and unhappy. Breaking these patterns leads to true authenticity, emotional freedom, and happiness. It is hard work but truly transformative.

In this book, the Eight Steps to Self-Awareness, Love, and Happiness come from my front-row experience with deep and lasting personal transformation in myself and in my clients.

I did not start off in coaching. I have been an entrepreneur all my life, from selling popcorn balls on the street corner as a kid to having my own successful graphic design/marketing business as an adult. In between businesses, I worked in corporate management, marketing and sales, and a variety of other industries. No matter what I did, I found myself helping people. I was a problem-solver extraordinaire! Whether I was mentoring someone at work or assisting clients with their personal situations, the joy I got from helping people gave me an inkling of my true calling.

But I had this warped idea about what happiness was. I thought if I could just become successful enough at my businesses and relationships, everything would fall into place and I would land myself a patch of nirvana and feel better. Meanwhile, I suffered, looking for the perfect answer to my imperfect life.

FROM BLAME TO ACCOUNTABILITY

I knew I needed professional help for my constant anxiety, my revolving yo-yo relationships, and the inner emptiness that haunted me. Like millions of others, I went to therapy and consulted with a variety of other healers. I became very good at articulating my problems and what I was doing to solve them. In fact, I got so good at intellectualizing my problems that one therapist I saw threw her hands up in the air and told me I was too evolved a being for her to help! It was disappointing, but looking back, I know that I brought it on myself. I knew how to talk the talk.

Each time I went to therapy, things would improve somewhat—but sooner or later I would find myself back in the dumps. I would feel relieved for a moment, and then the same thing would happen again. I could think through situations and know the right thing to do, but I kept falling back into my old patterns. Nothing seemed to work. I'd buy more books and seek out more help, but I still felt awful.

It was frustrating, but it also fueled my desire to feel better. One good trait of perfectionists and problem-solvers is we don't give up easily or settle for very long. My bigger insecurity was letting somebody know just how deep my soul-sucking insecurities ran. This I had to hide at all costs. I would have cringed had anyone known I did not have my act together.

One day, while walking down the street with ever-recurring problems on my mind, I experienced a major epiphany: I was, in fact, my own problem, a problem I could not solve in the way I had been trying to. I always thought information would be the answer. I always thought I did things the right way, and it was really others who would not cooperate. That day, I saw that I had never taken responsibility for my own choices and experiences. I was, in fact, a blamer!

This first epiphany was followed by a second, even more powerful one: I realized that until I got a clue about what was really going on inside of me emotionally, nothing outside of me would change. I saw how I had been avoiding my real emotions like they were the flu. No way had I been willing to scratch the scab on that wound!

These epiphanies hit me so hard that I had to catch my breath. I stopped walking, and standing on the sidewalk, I heard myself think, "You will work through your emotions until you can move on peacefully. Even if you want to run, avoid, or blame, you will stay with how you feel and not react out of old thinking. No more of this crap." I had no idea what the hell "staying with my feelings" entailed, but I eventually learned, and my life began to change.

This transformation took a long time—years. I found it mind-boggling trying to understand how to connect the dots between my intellectualizing, my perfectionist and people-pleasing behaviors, my poor choices, the abusive voice in my head, and my constant worry and suffering. Not only that, it was hard to see how truly awful I felt about myself. I recognized how little I understood the concept of self-love or how to apply it to myself. I just knew that I was never going to feel any different unless I took my epiphany seriously.

I was just beginning my coaching business and in yet another dysfunctional relationship I couldn't get right. I decided to use this on again/off again relationship to discover all the things *I was doing* that were causing me pain. Up until this point, I had really believed it was all him. *Why couldn't he get it right, so we could ride off into the sunset together?* Oh, brother, did I have a big corner to turn! Without holding my breath, I dove deep into the beliefs that propelled me to act in the dysfunctional ways I did. I needed to understand why I felt I wasn't worth much, even though I had achieved so much in my life. I continued to read a lot of self-help books, as I had done for years, but started to see how none of them could tell me *how* to change myself and be happy. Because of my epiphany, I knew that connecting to myself emotionally was the key.

It took many years of trial and error before I mastered this. I had to accept that I was screwed up, yet still lovable and wonderful. That sounded horrible. It also sounded impossible. But slowly, I noticed things about myself. Each time I got triggered into anxiety or other agonizing emotional states, I found that these emotions actually had very little to do with the situation at hand. Most of my feelings were from reactions specifically related to past experiences and the stories I had about them. I had to dive even deeper within myself, to a place beyond my surface reactionary emotions. This was tricky business, because how do you connect with something within yourself that you don't even know exists?

HOW I FINALLY GOT IT AND THE MAGIC BEGAN

My experiments with feeling my emotions and taking different types of action in my relationships and personal dramas became great tools in my coaching business. I was able to stop reacting to every picture hanging crookedly on the wall, because I realized my emotional issues were not solved by straightening up the artwork. As I became more empowered, I was able to bring what I was learning from my dysfunctional situations to help my clients with their dysfunctional situations.

Many of my clients had similar insecurities and, like me, they had become their own problems, suffering from the same patterns of people pleasing, looking for problems, assuming and personalizing (presuming that how people acted was about ME personally), and standing in the way of their own well-being. It was all they knew, as a way to be. Like me, many spent years believing if they just had the right strategy, it would somehow change their lives.

I showed them that strategy would not take them to a happier place—it was now about learning something new. It took a completely different approach to break them free of their BS, especially when it came to relationships. I came to see how insecure attachment issues drove their relationships, both personally and professionally.

As I did this work, I didn't just become happier, more empowered, and more emotionally available on the inside. I changed on the outside, too. I started attracting different men—men with self-awareness, who were interested in growing and becoming happier with themselves. I decided at one point that I was ready to open myself up to having a relationship with a life partner. A couple of months later, I met the man who would later be my husband. This relationship has been completely different from anything else I have ever experienced: it has been easy. The ease has come because I rooted out my negative beliefs and changed their patterns, and this altered my preconceived way of operating in the world.

Lasting change is possible. My life changed when I changed my perceptions of myself and opened up to what was possible for me. So can yours.

INTRODUCTION

You're Screwed Up, Lovable, and Wonderful

Today's society faces an epidemic of suffering from perfectionism, people pleasing, and related behaviors. We are bombarded with a standard of overdoing—whether overgiving, overworking, overcompensating, or overanalyzing. This compulsion to keep doing more doesn't stem from a happy place inside. It comes from negative beliefs about our own value, or lack thereof.

For many, the idea of perfectionism has been twisted into a positive thing; it means you are competitive, motivated, and always striving to be the best. For these perfectionists, suffering is something other, weaker people do. Most perfectionists, in fact, do not recognize their perfectionism as something harmful to themselves or to their relationships. This is the great irony of being perfect.

But be honest with yourself. *How happy are you?* Do you find yourself, for example, always running the race but never getting to the finish line, no matter how well you do, how hard you try, or whom you please? This is an exhausting and depleting way to live. Overdoing leads to burnout, anxiety, guilt, envy, and many other forms of suffering, including physical illness like hypertension.

As you read through this book, you will learn all the ways that being a stressed-out perfectionist, a burnt-out people pleaser, a frustrated problem-solver, or other painful conditions works against your lasting happiness and well-being. You will come to see how you got here through no fault of your own, because of something called "insecure attachment" in your childhood. You will see why becoming responsible for your choices, words, and actions as an adult can free you from the painful cons of perfectionism, people pleasing, and their compadres.

Prepare to become aware of what you may not have been able to see inside yourself before now. Learn about hidden forces affecting you, such as the insidious drama triangle (more on this on page 22), which wreaks havoc almost everywhere in our society as a major player in creating painfully repetitive relationship dynamics. It exerts a surprising influence on your expectations and what you find yourself reacting to, and it drives you to stay stuck right where you are.

As the influence of insecure attachment and the drama triangle become more transparent, you will be able to change the core of how you do things while becoming clear on your motivation behind the choices you make. The eight steps in this book will lead you to true self-awareness and happiness. You'll accept that you will never be perfect, but you can and will become the best you ever—screwed up, lovable, and wonderful.

PUTTING TOGETHER A PROCESS THAT WORKS

The most challenging part of developing a process for how to do this work is that it's emotional in nature, and emotions don't lend themselves well to linear processes. Instruction manuals are typically linear. You're given, say, steps one to five, with the promise that by the time you get to step five you will have put together your bicycle.

Dealing with our emotions is vastly different. Emotions ebb and flow, moving in more than one direction, with different intensities. They are always with us. And they really are our friends when we allow them to just be instead of avoiding them.

When you avoid, you store the emotion. It doesn't go away because you ignore it—quite the contrary. You choose to bury it, and it then affects your subconscious beliefs. Your beliefs were mainly created by the emotional impact of events happening around you, to you, and through you as a child. In effect, emotions influence you whether you want them to or not. Isn't it better to know them, rather than be surprised by them? Having awareness of your emotions makes it easier to release them. Developing a healthy relationship with your emotions is the key to changing your life.

THE EIGHT STEPS TO SELF-AWARENESS, LOVE, AND HAPPINESS

These steps are meant to unravel your unhappy behavioral patterns while at the same time building your self-value to a new normal. They come from over a decade of work in my personal life and my coaching experience with thousands of clients and podcast listeners just like you, who used these tools to change their lives.

You might have heard some of these steps in the past, but the difference here is in the approach. To actually break these unhappy behavioral patterns, you will come from an emotional perspective, which will require *feeling*, *courage*, *vulnerability*, and *action*. It will feel like learning a whole new language, and it is: the language of well-being.

The first six steps explore what you want to stop doing, and the last two steps identify what you want to start doing in your life. They each take you out of your comfort zone and invite you into the unknown within yourself. There may be times when you want to throw this book aside or light it on fire; these moments are prime opportunities for growth. Anything in this book that triggers an emotional reaction is an opportunity for you to change. This can feel super-challenging and scary at times, but I promise that if you persevere with the process, you will start to see change as your new best friend. Being stressed, upset, or demoralized by the beliefs that hold you back will be a thing of the past.

Here are the Eight Steps to Self-Awareness, Love, and Happiness:

STOP...

1. Avoiding your fears and attaching to outcomes

2. Trying to be perfect

3. People pleasing

4. Looking for problems to solve

5. Going against yourself as a victim/martyr (saying yes when you mean no, and vice versa)

6. Assuming and personalizing

START...

7. Taking responsibility

8. Feeling your true feelings

Starting in Chapter 4, you will be able to dive into the steps in depth, giving you a better understanding of why these patterns exist, what you believe they do for you, and how to break them. Don't skip the first three chapters, though—they are important in providing you with the tools you will need to take each step.

After you read the first three chapters, feel free to skip around through the chapters covering steps one through six. Those six steps are not written in linear fashion. Use a journal or notebook to write down your responses to the exercises and track the shifts and changes you find yourself going through as you progress through this book. Please set aside some quiet time while reading the book and reflecting on the work involved; you'll be glad you did. In fact, doing even one exercise will make you immediately feel better. The more exercises you do on a regular basis, the more you'll develop a completely different understanding of yourself and how you perceive life. You'll master your fears and step into your own power at the same time. I encourage rereading this book, because each time you do you will find a different aspect you may have missed the first time or discover you now see things differently.

This work of emotionally connecting to my authentic self is the most rewarding work I have ever done, and my hope is that you'll find it the same. It seems strange to say it, but I had no idea what well-being was before I began my journey of transformation. Now I do. My journey to happiness fuels my ability to zero in on others' self-generated obstacles and help them make the only shift that matters in the end: the shift from head to heart. The hard work of dropping your emotional armor and kicking your anxiety to the curb will lead you to true self-acceptance, emotional freedom, a more authentic life, and happiness.

CHAPTER 1

Insecure Attachment and the Drama Triangle

HOW CAN YOU BE THE PROBLEM?

It may be hard to see yourself as your own problem. It may be shocking, because you identify yourself as "having it together"—you always excel in some way. Perhaps you're an overachiever, an overgiver, a "Dear Abby," or a control freak (it's cute, right?). You might think, "This is who I am. I've worked hard to get here. I have my act together. It's everyone else."

In fact, the last thing you want is for others to find out you're not this perfectly amazing person all the time. What? You might be screwed up like the rest of us? You might very well have worked your ass off to get to this place of appearing good enough that no one will criticize you or find fault with you. You might wear a coating of Teflon—"Don't mess with me!"—or be Mother Teresa's stand-in.

If so, you know that it takes a lot of work, and things are never perfect. Even if you try to do everything right, the tulips keep coming up crabgrass. This standoff with life causes you distress and anxiety. You just keep trying harder, thinking harder, working harder for that solution that eludes you. You've read every self-help book under the sun!

Maybe you're married, but you and your spouse are leading separate lives, cheating, or constantly at each other's throats. Or you tell your partner again and again how you want to be closer with them, but it never happens; emotional distance is a fact of your history. Avoiding emotions altogether could be your calling card, if you've been single for the past decade. Not happily single, but having given up, becoming numb and telling yourself all the endeavors, friends, and little critters you have are good enough. Nothing you do seems to change your outcomes, your relationships, or the patterns in your life.

The reason your life is at a stalemate is because you are not seeing yourself accurately. You think you have your act perfectly together, but you have problems all over the place. If you fear being outed as less than the picture you portray, you obsess over every little detail gone wrong, blaming everything and everyone around you when life does not go your way: "My boss gave me the wrong instructions!" or "I followed the recipe, it's total crap!"

You are not living with FOMO (fear of missing out) but FIFO (fear I'm found out). The people in your life can't know anything about the screwed-up you. What if they used it against you? Stopped loving you? Stopped thinking the world of the amazing you? How would you feel without that validation from others?

If you were to see yourself accurately, you'd come to see that *you* are really your problem. Your perfectionist, people-pleasing, problem-solving ways; your need for control, fear of being found out, insistence on having your way, unhappiness with others—all of this is on you.

If you're confused about how you affect your own life and why things look as they do, you're not alone. Knowing what you are doing intellectually can still leave you unaware of what you are doing emotionally, physically, and verbally.

In the old days, I'd break off a romance with someone who I felt wasn't meeting my needs. My needs ranged from dictating our dating schedule to having a partner commit to me in my time frame. At the time, I had no idea why this was important to me. All I knew was that I was trying hard, and I was making sacrifices for him with my time and commitment, so I expected the same from him. Whatever he did or did not do, I seemed to overreact. I did not like feeling bad, needy, or out of control, and I expected the guy to fix it. In trying to control how I felt and change him, too, I would break up with him to win my way. The idea was to make him afraid of losing me. So, in a dramatic fashion, I'd expect him to make me promises based on my being right and him being the problem child.

Can you say bad strategy? Never mind that it did not really work. I felt full of anxiety all the time. If it were the game of Battleship, I would've lost all my ships. I could not see that controlling, pushing, arguing, and oscillating between being a helpless victim and a rescuer was not solving my problem. All I did was react and go down the dark rabbit hole of self-loathing. I felt like I was losing my marbles. I kept at it for years. Part of me truly believed that if I bugged a man about his flaws or bought him enough books, it would all work out in my favor.

As a human being, it is hard to see yourself clearly. Other people may offer opinions or criticisms, but they never really capture what is happening inside of us at a deeper level. Often, it is only through seeing how we react to life that we gain any knowledge of ourselves and see that our reactions come straight from our conditioned preferences. We may believe that these preferences are a truth, but they are just habits.

The key is to learn why you have the preference. You have a deeper motivation as you go through daily life, one that has nothing to do with your reactions but everything to do with why you have a reaction in the first place. This motivation comes from how you felt about past events, and from your perception of yourself in those events. For example, you might hate being stuck in the rain without an umbrella, because of what happened when you were drenched before an important event in your life. Therefore, you always have the umbrella with you—even on sunny days. Your motivation drives your behavior. Without knowing your motivations, you can't know yourself.

Paying attention to what you do and why you do it will give you some insight into how you are the biggest barrier to your own happiness. Your feelings impact your thoughts, and your thoughts impact your feelings. How you see a situation outside of your body impacts both your thoughts and your feelings. You then have a reaction to it. You do this throughout the day about a variety of things. Take a moment and scan how many reactions you have in a day, whether to other people or to situations beyond your control. If you pay attention, you might notice yourself making judgments about everyone you meet.

Most of this mental chatter is not something you actively notice, but it does impact you. You might also notice that you get uptight. This tension or anxiety is a reaction, too. When you pay deeper attention, rather than drawing conclusions established from tension, you might notice other feelings, too—possibly even pain.

Seeing your own reactions to daily life is the first step toward solving your problems. Before you can take the road to happiness, you must first discover where you are.

WHAT INSECURE ATTACHMENT MEANS FOR YOU

As a baby, you didn't choose your parents. It was not like you could flip through a catalog for the perfect parents. You went home with your primary caregiver. Some of them were not very self-aware; in fact, they may have bordered on abusive or been outright abusive, dismissive, or anxious. Or they may have attached to you in an overprotective manner. The deal is, they may have screwed you up a little bit. It's not anything you can't reverse when it comes to painful conditioning. That's why you're reading this book. In this book, being screwed up is like being a cool kid, because you are the star, and now you are moving on to a whole new script.

One thing to understand about insecure attachment or the other concepts discussed in this book is that they are all just conditioning. You learned these counterproductive ways of avoiding happiness long ago. The good news is that because you learned it, you can unlearn it, too.

Attachment is one of many facets of parenting. It describes an aspect of the emotional relationship between a parent and child. A securely attached child feels assured that his or her caregiver will meet their needs. In 1969, psychologist John Bowlby developed the theory of attachment. He suggested that early childhood attachment to caregivers gives a child the foundation for their self-worth and their feelings of importance and consistency in relationships, intimate and otherwise.

So, your parents either provided you with a secure base or an insecure base, and this established your own models for how the world works, emotionally. In 1970, Mary Ainsworth, a psychologist who teamed up with Bowlby, followed up his theory with an experiment of her own, called the "Strange Situation." The Strange Situation involved mothers and their infants, who were between the ages of 9 and 18 months. Over eight sessions, the children were either left alone in a room, with their mother, with a stranger, or with their mother and a stranger. As their mothers left and reunited with the children, their reactions were observed and their attachment styles noted, along with other behaviors. This experiment led her to suggest that securely attached children would respect themselves and their needs, while insecurely attached children would feel unworthy because they had developed a negative self-image. Psychologists theorized that attachment styles would continue to affect how children emotionally adjusted through adolescence and into early adulthood. These early life patterns are what you may have carried forth into your adult life.

Well wait, couldn't I be a securely attached kid?

Maybe. Secure attachment permits children to trust others, themselves, and what life brings. These kids have the secure foundation needed to discover, bond, and openly communicate with others. They grow up with a strong sense of well-being, motivation, and safety. Having this base gives them a feeling of trust. They are not initially suspicious, wondering what a person wants from them. These kids aren't doing a balancing act on a cup while juggling bowling pins for attention. They feel confident in how they assess the world and their place in it.

This ability to trust makes a huge difference when it comes to handling change. These children are able to adapt, cope with stress, and be emotionally resilient. All of this adds up to a solid foundation for building emotional intelligence. Securely attached kids more easily gain the four branches of emotional intelligence identified by John Mayer and Peter Salovey in 1990. Mayer and Salovey were the first to create a framework in exploring and defining an emotional intelligence with four branches, as follows: first, the ability to perceive emotions in oneself and others accurately; second, the ability to use emotions to facilitate thinking; third, the ability to understand emotions, emotional language, and the signals conveyed by emotions; and fourth, the ability to manage emotions toward a goal.

By providing attention and recognizing their children's material and emotional needs, securely attached parents lay a strong foundation for self-esteem in their kids. Trust, empathy, understanding relationships, and knowing how verbal and nonverbal communication work come easily to these kids.

Sounds great! Sign me up!

Now, let's take a short walk to the other side of the street, which could be your side of the street.

Here's the down low on insecure attachment: inconsistencies in the actions/reactions of a caregiver will affect the quality of attachment in the child, especially actions and reactions that are repetitive behaviors. Perhaps a parent, or both Mom and Dad, were fundamentally dysfunctional because of their own upbringing. Maybe one or both were emotionally distant, or maybe they were emotionally dependent on you, the child. Yes, right up in your business! Maybe they did not trust you to decide on anything you really wanted, and/or they overprotected you, living your life for you and shielding you from all disappointment. You would not have learned how to deal with life on life's terms. Or perhaps you lost a parent or both parents early in life. Even an extended stay in the hospital for you or a parent, or a job where they weren't around much, would affect your style of attachment.

If they were clueless as parents, you didn't learn much in the areas of boundaries or emotional safety, either. Basically, they caused you considerable emotional distress and you needed to find a way to survive, so you got your own map and compass together. You learned to avoid your emotions, because they felt hard and painful. Negative feelings can be big, even overwhelming, to a little body. So "fuhgeddaboudit" to those old emotions! Phooey, who needs 'em? You found safety in a rejecting environment by building defensive mental strategies, which relieved frustration and pain and toned down your intense emotional states.

Now, before I continue, let me point out that this book is not about blaming Mom or Dad. The point in understanding attachment is to give you a clearer idea of where your problem started, how it has affected you, and how to resolve it.

As an insecurely attached child, you might have been inconsolable much of the time, rejecting of your parent, or you might have turned yourself into a self-contained little adult. That's what I did, and my mom called me her "little soldier." If your childhood was like mine, your main strategy to protect yourself might have been to never do something as dangerous as showing any desire or need for closeness, warmth, affection, or love. Crying in movie theaters or in front of others was very scary; it attracted the wrong attention. You still wanted to be physically close to your parent, but you became emotionally detached. You needed validation but couldn't get it from the dysfunctional parent, so you sought it in school, through friends, or in other ways. You knew that you had to go elsewhere to gain a feeling of belonging and acceptance.

Even as very young children, we insecurely attached kids had to learn to sidestep our troublesome feelings as we caught on that our caregivers showed little or no interest in truly getting to know us or understand how we felt. This left us with a bottomless pit of emptiness inside. I was that kid!

We carried these strategies into adulthood, and now the reality of getting emotionally close to others can have us breaking out in a cold sweat. We think that getting close to others emotionally should come with a guarantee that no one will get hurt or be left out, but that's a fantasy. A lot of us insecurely attached children end up single our entire lives or settling for unfulfilling relationships, never sure if we made the right choice or feeling we had no choice. The emptiness inside is pervasive. We become gifted at developing strategies for both getting attention and avoiding attention altogether.

Strategies can be helpful in business when it comes to developing goals, but not so much for getting love and attention. In fact, we may end up being quite successful in our work, gaining validation and allowing us to keep our emotional distance with the world. For many, insecure attachment meant your intellect took over and saved the day. You got through by striving for something beyond just being you. You might have become an overachiever, a high performer, or a people pleaser, doing whatever you could to avoid negative consequences. You got your act together and you kept it together! But does being in this type of control serve you now? How happy are you?

If you were insecurely attached as a child, you can't grasp what it feels like to be responsible for how you feel. It's not your fault. It's your conditioning. You never learned, so you don't have the right tools. You may not know how to take emotionally inspired action, or how to stop being in a state of reaction to life and the people in it. Whether you anxiously run toward what you believe will fill you up or appear to avoid it, you have the same result: lack of real connection, happiness, and love.

Here's the deal: To get to the other side of the street as an adult, you want to see yourself as the place where all your answers reside. All of them are inside of you. Trust that you will learn how to stop seeking problems outside of yourself, along with all the other behaviors you've used to avoid your own answers. Let's start here, today, with "you are screwed up (and it's okay)." You are your own answer now!

CHOOSING TO SUFFER IN THE DRAMA TRIANGLE: FROM VICTIM TO RESCUER TO MARTYR TO VILLAIN

Now, let's pull back the veil to see what else is going on. The drama triangle, also known as the Karpman Drama Triangle, explains a lot. In fact, you will see the drama triangle not only in your own life, but everywhere! It's in movies, songs, TV shows, your friends' relationships, and so on. It is a socially acceptable way to be dysfunctional.

What is it?

Originally introduced in 1968 in "Fairy Tales and Script Drama Analysis," by Stephen B. Karpman, MD, the Karpman Drama Triangle is an upside-down triangle with three positions on it. In the upper-left corner is the persecutor, in the upper-right corner is the rescuer, and in the bottom is the victim. Several variations have emerged; my own variation is that the rescuer is also the martyr, because each is the flipside of the other.

What do the points on the triangle mean in relation to this work?

The triangle represents the dynamics we have unconsciously chosen to participate in, in relation to others. It shows how the balance of power shifts between people in conflict and points out how individuals show up to interact in daily life. All three points on the triangle illustrate a lack of personal responsibility when in a struggle with other people.

Unfortunately, these points on the triangle are not only dysfunctional, they are emotionally draining and potentially harmful to those involved. Those who find themselves cruising on the triangle will shift positions, depending on the situation, without even realizing it. The victim feels they need a persecutor and someone to rescue them. Needing someone and being disrespected by them at the same time causes some victims to become the persecutor, but then, feeling bad, they want to rescue the person they just persecuted.

Going from each of the positions—from persecutor to rescuer to victim, in any order—makes it difficult to know what you are doing. You don't know why you're doing it, either, because you learned the motivations for these positions in childhood and are on autopilot.

You decide you want things to be a specific way, and maybe you ask for it: "I want us to leave for our vacation on Friday night instead of Saturday morning." Let's say you don't get what you want. What do you do? The victim feels sorry for themselves; the persecutor may bully others to comply, or rail at the other person in an attempt to make them feel bad; the rescuer feels they must try harder by fixing or coming across as altruistic, as though asking for what they want is free of ego.

The drama triangle supplies an undercurrent of dysfunction and disempowerment as these dynamics run rampant in, around, and through our lives. Everyone on it is a prisoner until they can see it at the level of self-awareness. Until there is awareness, being on the drama triangle allows each participant to avoid addressing the real issues.

What does the persecutor do on this triangle? Think of the villain in movies, the one jerk in a reality TV show, or even the person being sung to in a love song. Have you ever noticed how sad love songs are? Most of them are about being left by someone, aka the persecutor, because the singer (victim) feels powerless to change anything. The persecutor is seen as the one with the power, even though it is not true power. Who wears the pants in the family? The persecutor. Who is the bully, the one who blames, shows anger in a domineering manner, and is overly critical and outwardly controlling? The persecutor again. Got a boss who rips you apart all the time? You feel like they are the persecutor. Does your partner tell you what to do when it comes to how you need to live "their" life, so they will be happy with you? That's the persecutor. The person who cheated on you and left you high and dry? The persecutor strikes again!

How about the rescuer on the triangle? What is he or she up to? The rescuer/fixer/martyr is so enmeshed in other people that he or she has no clue how they feel themselves or what they truly want. It is always about other people. They avoid themselves and mask it by being overly concerned for the victim. Their seemingly altruistic care of others is rarely seen as controlling by the people they rescue. But rescuers keep a scorecard in their head of everything they do for others, and through this scorecard a sense of superiority develops. (This is also how they end up as the persecutor at some point—when they finally flip out.) This person is the enabler of bad behavior. He or she will help you out when you're stuck in a foreign country; though you're barely acquaintances, they will fly there and pick you up! No task is too much or too big, as long as they receive the reward of validation. The validation, of course, lasts only so long. It doesn't fill them up. In essence, a rescuer is pretty angry, thinking, "I do everything for everyone, but no one does anything for me." The truth is that rescuers do want rescuing, but they appear to be self-sufficient, so no one believes they need any help. To actually receive help would make them feel weak, or shame, and they do not want to owe anyone in return. In contrast, the rescuer wants the victim to have ESP to fulfill their needs in a way that doesn't disrupt their superior position. It's a double-edged sword, because they only feel validation or power when rescuing. Rescuers on the surface don't think they need any help, because inevitably "they have it handled."

Now we come to the victim. Victims are talked about so much in society, but there are many types of victims running around this planet. This is the most powerless position on the surface, but underneath the apparent passivity is manipulation. The victim throws themselves regular pity parties but also feels persecuted by others with sentiments like "I'd rather be alone"; "I hate men/women"; "They are all jerks!" or "Poor me, nobody does anything for me"; "I'm all alone"; "Nobody cares"; and "No one would miss me if I were gone." This position is inwardly controlling. Anyone who believes their emotional state is controlled by someone else is a victim. For example, a victim might say, "I can't believe you are not taking me out on a Friday night just because you have to work late. I'm feeling like you don't care. You owe me."

How else does the victim position show up? They panic about making a decision for fear someone won't like it. They ask others for their opinion about a decision they are contemplating in their life. They act like they don't care, but inside they feel victimized by others. A victim complains they are never chosen or says things like they are not attractive or interesting enough. Whenever you feel powerless, hopeless, defeated, ashamed, or depleted and you blame another person, you're a victim.

Victims have no empowerment, but they get a different type of power from wallowing in their misery. This power is to guilt-trip the world—they don't have to be responsible for anyone or anything. Moving into the "victim" spot on the triangle can be a relief because no one expects anything from you.

No one on the drama triangle is taking responsibility or practicing any kind of self-care. They are all waiting for something outside themselves to make them take action, which is really a reaction. It's a reaction because another person doing something to upset them is what gets the party started on the triangle. When living on this triangle, we find it impossible to be authentic. Each position wants to win.

Look at how society is obsessed with reality TV, soap operas, and generally watching other people's drama unfold like it's a train wreck. We get drawn in because we love watching the drama of others. Our own drama? Not so much, but you'll buy tickets to the movie to see the good guy (rescuer) trying to save the damsel in distress (victim) by battling the bad guy (persecutor). It's a classic format we've seen over and over again. Think *Bridget Jones's Diary*, with Hugh Grant (persecutor), Colin Firth (rescuer), and Renée Zellweger (victim). In the TV show *South Park*, Cartman is a victim, persecutor, and rescuer all built into one little dude. He can be a bully but then feels picked on so he runs to his mom (or anyone who will listen), and then he and his gang of friends are often rescuing someone.

We watch this form of entertainment because it's familiar; we know the dynamic well. We have been conditioned to think this way since childhood, so we don't see another way. We want a winner and a loser. A good guy and a bad guy. And we want to cheer for the rescuer.

It's entertainment, but in real life, it's painful. It's inauthentic and depleting. The opposite of the drama triangle is happiness and empowerment,

                Overcoming Insecure Attachment

but we don't see that as an option... unless that happiness is dependent on someone else.

EXERCISE: Recognizing the Drama Triangle

To recognize the drama triangle in your own life, take the time while you're reading this book to notice and pay attention to popular culture. Watch TV shows to see if you can identify the different roles and how people switch positions on the triangle. Society is a reflection of the people in it, and by seeing the drama triangle outside yourself, you'll be able to see yourself more clearly.

Then, take a few minutes to journal your answers to the following questions:

1. What do you now notice that you might not have observed in the past? Are you able to see how disempowering the drama triangle dynamic is?

2. Now, turn that awareness on your own life and look at where *you* play each of these roles on the triangle. I guarantee you do it. Take a few minutes to sketch out the triangles you're aware of at work, at home, and with friends.

3. The next time you catch yourself in one of the drama triangle positions, *stop* and ask yourself what you're trying to force. Most people don't even know the motivation for what they're trying to accomplish. Consider what could happen if you dropped your role and just let the situation unfold. If you are trying to get someone to do what you want so you can feel better, stop trying to get that from them. Instead, give it to yourself. That is the beginning of empowerment.

EMOTIONAL BAGGAGE—CAN YOU LEAVE IT AT THE AIRPORT?

Your emotional baggage goes wherever you go. It's hard to unpack because often you cannot see it. It's invisible luggage, but it affects everything. You might not know how heavily it weighs on your view of life.

Imagine having an empty backpack as a kid. Little by little, events happen in your life, and the backpack starts to fill. Some of these events impact you emotionally. Remember what happened when little Johnny was running with scissors? He fell and cut himself. It required stitches. And guaranteed, little Johnny remembers that event and feels a shock of fear down his spine in recalling it. It probably curtailed any possibility of a career as a professional sword swallower. Not only that, but his backpack then had some weight to it.

Your baggage starts to fill up as your view of the world changes based on how your experiences impact you, creating a reaction. What you used to be able to do now scares the crap out of you, so you run, hide, overcompensate, or do magic tricks to prevent the event from happening again. You may not understand why, but geez, that backpack is feeling heavier! And you can't see how it is impacting your choices.

Heavy baggage means you developed a belief about yourself and the world. Attachment issues, modeling the people you knew who were enthusiastic participants on the drama triangle—all of this told you things about the world and your own place in it. Whenever a negative event happened, it created a negative belief, a belief you fed over and over. The fear of that negative belief being true is part of why your baggage feels so heavy.

Seeking perfection, being a people pleaser, or having other depleting traits comes from a heavy emotional backpack. You might work really hard to ignore the weight of it, hoping that all the over-the-top things you do, like going 30 miles out of your way to pick up your friend's dress from the dry cleaner even though you have your own errands to run, will make it lighter. Instead, you find yourself overreacting to little things, wondering afterward what got into you. It's those moments of overreaction that provide clues into your emotional baggage.

And believe me, you want clues! You want to drop that stuff like it's a grenade. Emotional baggage can be difficult to tackle because to clear it, you need to know it's there. And even when you know it's there, a large part of clearing it means taking responsibility for the choices you made when you unconsciously stuffed more into the backpack. The good news is that you don't have to continue to see the world from the same screwed-up place. You do not have to make the same choices in the future.

A new age guy I was dating years ago said to me, "It's always about the p**sy. Once you have sex, then they want everything from you." This was his irritated response to my saying it would be great to see him a couple of times a week. I was shocked by Mr. Meditation and took it personally, shutting down and screaming in my head, "What is wrong with me?!" I'll spare you the gory details of how this scenario played out, but it added to my emotional baggage. For a long time afterward, I never said what I wanted when it came to seeing a man on a regular basis. I was afraid of having another response out of left field. I did not feel worthy of someone wanting to see me regularly. This related right back to my heavy-ass backpack, even though I did not realize it. I just thought that men really did not want a serious relationship with me. (I still thought Mr. Meditation was a jerk.) Ugh. Feels heavy reading it, doesn't it?

Any time you were given evidence that your screwed-up belief was true, your emotional baggage grew. Whether you shut down, freaked out, or tried to convince yourself and others things were different is irrelevant. It made no impact on the size of your emotional baggage. As it grew into a full-on trunk, you avoided situations that you feared could bring up that evidence again. You ran away emotionally. You probably became more perfect, so no one would find out that you were a loser (I don't think this—*you* do, and that's why you are your own problem). Feeling that specific events or that certain people, places, things, and situations are the problem keeps you from dealing with your baggage.

So, are you ready to off-load some of your non–Louis Vuitton luggage and get on down the road to happiness? Get ready to move from auto-pilot to feeling your feelings and the beginnings of emotional freedom.

CHAPTER 2

How Your Lizard Brain Runs You

WHAT IS THE LIZARD BRAIN?

Your lizard brain cares only about survival. The lizard brain, also known as the limbic system, is the oldest part of the brain. According to science, it reacts to fear with the urge to fight or flight. This ancient part of your brain also houses your basic needs, like those for food, sex, and love. It is where many emotional and mental processes are born, and it is part of your subconscious mind.

Ever wonder why you react or feel compelled to keep doing things the same way over and over? It's your lizard brain. It stays in control, like an overly protective parent who is afraid for your safety, saying, "Watch out for that car!" Even if you complain about your circumstances, your biology says, "This is safe," so it can feel difficult to change. Repetition matters to the lizard brain. Every time you do things in the same way, it knows you are alive. It keeps barbed wire in the form of fear around any type of change. You may not even understand the connection between fear and what you do because the lizard brain is behind the curtain, acting like the Wizard of Oz.

It's why stopping a habit like smoking, breaking up a dysfunctional relationship, or losing weight can be hard. Your lizard brain sees these situations as familiar and does not want to change the scenario because it wants you alive. See the contradiction here? It doesn't give a hoot if you are happy. The lizard brain isn't invested in the details of your deepest desires; it just cares that you are standing upright and breathing. The best way for it to operate is to keep what you do on autopilot, like driving a car, riding a bike, or brushing your teeth—it *prefers* that you do not notice what's going on under the radar. The autopilot process extends to how you react and what you react to: "What do you mean I just tried to run someone off the road? I don't have road rage!" Autopilot makes it difficult to have self-awareness.

It's this autopilot way of living that has brought you to this standoff with life. When you get up each day, your thoughts are often the same thoughts you had the day before, unless something new has plopped itself down in your life. Even then, your thoughts may still be the same kind of thoughts. As you go about your day, notice how your thoughts and feelings feel the same. You may feel uptight and not know why as you picture getting ready for work, going through traffic, and being at your job. It is a state of repetition. You react to the same thoughts and feelings, but you don't go deeper to see why you do what you do or think what you think. It's *Groundhog Day*. Routine is safe to the lizard brain. As long as you are distracted from what is going on inside of you at a deeper level, it knows you will do and think what is familiar.

If your emotional needs weren't met when you were a child, clearly you wouldn't have felt safe. You would have felt a certain emptiness or insecurity. If Mom or Dad shut you down emotionally—ignored you, belittled you, or over-protected you—you will have an emotional safety issue. Your subconscious will be on the constant lookout for danger. It wants to spot the first sign of trouble, so it can jump into action and protect you. This is great if you're walking down a dark alley, but constantly assessing your surroundings to make sure everything is under control so that you stay safe is exhausting. It can make you quite the detective, looking for clues in what others say and do, especially clues to where things might go wrong!

Do a little experiment here. Stop reading for a minute and ask yourself, "What am I thinking about? What am I focused on? Is it me?"

Nope! It's something else, right? Pay attention to how focusing on something outside yourself feels. Then take the experiment one step further: What feelings accompany what you focus on? Look for the connection... is there one? You may not feel anything, and that is okay. I really want you to notice the absence of focus on yourself. Now here is a good trick. Switch your focus to your stomach. Really focus on your stomach and see what happens. Notice the difference? It *feels* different. You may not know what the feeling is, but it has a different feeling, right? If you've been scratching your head over why things aren't changing inside of you—now you know it's because you've been focusing outside of yourself. You aren't giving any attention to your inner world.

One of the reasons many self-help books or self-help workshops do not work for long is that your same old thoughts and perceptions take in the information intellectually. The information sounds good, as though it may finally provide the answer to your woes—until, of course, life happens. When life happens, the ol' lizard brain kicks right back into gear, and pretty soon you find yourself reacting in the same old way: "I am so good at meditating, but I yelled at my boyfriend for leaving his bowl in the sink!" The technique of feeling your reactions, which I'll address in this book, will help you to take a major step toward changing this dynamic in yourself so your out-of-the-blue freak-outs will be minimal, if they happen at all.

Another aspect of the lizard brain is the incessant chatter of that voice in your head telling you what an idiot you are. Words such as the following work as another form of protection to keep you safe: "You're such an asshole"; "Who does that?!" and "I can't believe you just said that to her!" This type of chatter is demeaning and shaming, but how is it protective?

The part of your brain trying to keep you safe wants you to hear loud and clear when you screw up that your behavior is somehow a threat to your safety. Your mistake threatens the norm you operate in, so your lizard brain wants you to stop whatever it was you did or might do. Does that mean the situation is actually threatening? No. The lizard brain doesn't know the difference between a true threat and an emotional one, because fear feels the same in the body.

Years ago, my former business partner was fed up with me and wanted to know what drove me to be a workaholic. I had never looked inside myself. But somehow, a flicker of a lightbulb went off this time, and I saw how I was still trying to be like my dad. My mom always told me as a kid that I was like him and that if they ever got divorced, I would go live with him. Underlying all my actions was the message, "You are just like your dad." She said we deserved each other. My relationship with him wasn't great because he wasn't around much, and when he was, he was pretty distracted. I rarely got his positive attention. I felt somewhat proud that my mother accused me of being like him because he seemed successful in the pursuit of his work and he had the greatest sense of humor. In my work ethic, I was trying to gain the acceptance he had denied me by living according to his beliefs about success.

Clearly, I was still unacceptable in my own mind, as my little lizard brain had me working like a dog. Between my workaholicism and my relentless inner critic, I was an asshole to myself. It never brought me any closer to acceptance or improved anything in terms of happiness or feeling good. Even after that lightbulb moment, I kept up that same pattern for years. Although I saw that my motivation came from wanting to be like my dad, I did not understand how to stop. I was on autopilot, surviving rather than looking deeper into how to change or move out of my self-destructive habits.

Just like me, you and everybody else learned how to survive through examples from your family, friends, classmates, or society. Your lizard brain kept track of all this information and set up the many rules of how you were to engage with life. As long as you were alive and the outside looked good, your subconscious was doing its job.

Maybe you think this is all BS. So what if you focus on controlling the world to stay safe, or if your inner critic is a dickhead who never shuts up? Hey, guess what? Allowing the world to fearfully control your mood and 'tude will not bring you to the end of the rainbow. It's not what will make you happy.

I'd like to bring a bit of science into it. Many of the studies done on happy people focus on a "locus of control," or the degree to which people believe they have control over the events that impact their lives. Those with an internal locus of control not only believe "this too shall pass," but also that they have control over their lives. Not over other people and outside events, but over their own actions and reactions. They believe that things, for the most part, will work out for the best. They have a solid sense of well-being and are not picking up a bunch of emotional drama to stuff into their backpack. They feel fairly safe and secure most of the time. Their lizard brain is not shouting orders 24/7 with an inner critic as the chorus.

In contrast, those with an external locus of control feel unsafe all the time. They feel that no matter what they do, the result is up to fate.

Any time you rely on the outside to make your insides feel okay, you are looking for trouble. Up until now, you might have had your fear on autopilot, unchecked. You can change the balance of power inside of you so that your lizard brain is not leading the charge in trying to control what you see, think, and believe. Having awareness about your lizard brain—and the fear it operates from—will change how you feel and what you do.

NEGATIVE BELIEFS CREATE PATTERNS TO MAKE THEM TRUE!

The easiest way to stay alive is to maintain certain patterns controlling your behavior and your choices. Patterns have been a means of survival since early humans walked the earth: patterns of nature, patterns of the solar system, patterns of other people. We watched the saber-toothed tiger from our caves, noticing its hunting patterns at dusk. He scared us each time we saw him because he had our neighbor's dad for breakfast one day. That emotional impact left a splat on our belief system. "I am going to die if I go outside," we thought. From that point on, the pattern was to avoid not just the tiger but also the dusk.

Human beings look for patterns all around themselves, but rarely inside of themselves. You don't observe your own patterns unless you see something you are experiencing over and over as a source of frustration (and not always then).

You designed these patterns. You probably don't remember doing it because it was a long time ago. Patterns were formed from your belief system, which is housed in your subconscious and is a part of your lizard brain. Patterns are a way of gaining evidence through your actions and words that your belief is true. If you believe you're going to lose the baseball game, your patterns will do what they can to support that belief. Imagine: You miss the fly ball and you start psyching yourself out that you will strike out before you even get up to bat. And guess what? You strike out!

Patterns on autopilot keep the belief from being challenged. If you can't connect (or even see) the dots and see the motivation behind your patterns, you'll keep doing the same things. When faced with negative circumstances, your patterns may also keep you continually blaming the outside world: "The universe always screws me over!" You walk into all situations with this "survival instinct" leading the way rather than being open to a new experience: "I already know my boss is a jerk in staff meetings!"; "Whenever I walk in the door after work the house is chaos with my kids, husband, and even the dog!"; "I am so tired, give me a break!"; "He never calls me after six p.m., and it makes me angry!" You cannot see how your patterns have blinders on, keeping you frustrated on this merry-go-round of hell.

How did your pesky negative patterns stemming from nonthreatening circumstances come about? You know, those like needing to be perfect and hiding who you really are? The good old belief system is basically what shapes your perception and behavior. It is the motivation behind your patterns, both positive and negative.

As a kid, you repeated emotional reactions to events happening to you or around you. Like a video camera, your lizard brain recorded this information. It interpreted these emotional events as meaningful. Your reaction to the event, combined with the repetition of the event, created a belief: "This always happens to me!"

Beliefs also come from your parents and society. You probably learned some of your negative beliefs by getting in trouble or some other negative event, which stuck with you emotionally. Your beliefs are always gathering evidence in your daily life, proving themselves true, even if you work your tail off trying to nullify them. Why do they prove themselves true? It is the basis of your survival as a species. If you believe there is ground beneath your feet, you keep walking; but what if you believed your next step was an endless ravine? If you believed it, then it would be hard to talk you out of the belief, no matter how ridiculous it seemed. Politics, anyone?

Let's say you were yelled at as a child for being bad and it felt painful. You didn't like feeling bad, so you recorded a negative belief about pain being bad. You also created a negative belief that *you* are bad. You developed a positive belief that being perfect was a way to escape being yelled at, so you would avoid pain.

Fast forward to your life as an adult, where you go about on autopilot, setting up evidence to support the belief that you are bad. At the same time, you also carried into your adult life the belief that pain is bad and being perfect is good. So, you do things you think would be perfectly good. You overcompensate, trying to be perfect. You exhaust yourself and probably have for years, but since it's your norm, you may not even know how tired you are in the pursuit of being perfect. In the end, no matter how much overcompensating you do, the evidence for "I am bad" always wins. (You're not really bad or good, you're just lovably screwed up.)

My client Lisa was seven years old when she got the idea to help out by cleaning the house. Her perfectionist tendencies had already kicked into gear at this point. She was trying to do something nice to gain approval. She cleaned thoroughly, even throwing out a scrap of fabric that belonged to her stepmother. To her surprise, her stepmother was furious. Apparently, the fabric had been important—a swatch for recovering the sofa. She yelled at Lisa for being inconsiderate, and Lisa shut down. She grew confused about good and bad because she didn't understand what she had done wrong. She had tried hard to be perfect to gain acceptance and love, but it didn't work. To her, the scrap had looked like a piece of trash—an honest mistake for a seven-year-old.

Through our sessions, Lisa recalled other times when her actions had been misunderstood, truly backfiring, especially when she was over-compensating and trying to be perfect or do the right thing. These experiences led her to develop the belief that she couldn't do things right and was therefore a bad person. They filled her emotional back-pack to the breaking point.

As an adult, Lisa continued working hard to be perfect. She needed the validation of being told by others that she was okay. She did every-thing she could for them so they would not discover her fatal flaw of always doing things wrong. Worse yet, her feelings did not matter as long as she could avoid feeling the pain of rejection or of disappoint-ing someone else. She overcompensated constantly, burning herself out. Inevitably, all her efforts would hit a wall, and something would unexpectedly slip through the cracks—she would feel found out and those old shameful feelings would rush in again. She was always bad and misunderstood in her own mind. She could not see her beliefs and patterns—they were totally hidden underneath what she believed was true.

As we worked together, Lisa became much kinder to herself, did not overcompensate as much, changed some of her beliefs enough to relax, made different choices, got into a relationship with a really great guy, and found a much better life for herself!

If, like Lisa, you've been working hard to be good, accepted, and perhaps perfect, the belief system you have exists in a land of pain. It tells you that you need to be "good enough" to gain love, acceptance, and whatever else is meaningful to you. You don't realize that a lot of your behavior is driven by this pain. You allow pain to be in the driver's seat because it is comfortable to your lizard brain—it's familiar. It's what the evidence has shown you, feeding into what you believe about yourself and the world. But you won't magically wake up and experience goodness and wholeness by continuing this pattern.

Here is a short list of some of the most common negative beliefs. There are many more, but it always comes back to some form of a lack of self-worth. You can try some of them on for size. You will know if it feels true, because some event that has happened in your life will come to mind, reminding you of that feeling inside that says, "Yep, that's me!"

Negative core beliefs include:

- I don't deserve money, love, happiness, etc.
- I'm not good enough to be promoted, to have a mate, to be chosen, etc.
- I'm meant to be alone (I am alone, no one wants me, I always get left).

- I'm worthless (I lost my job, I made a mistake, I can't do anything right).
- I'm a failure (I worked my ass off and lost it all, I will never be successful).
- I'm invisible (I make no impact on the world, no one can see the real me).
- I have nothing to offer (I do nothing, so no one owes me; I'm irresponsible).
- There's something wrong with me (I'll be found out and abandoned, I am horrible).
- I'm unlovable (I'm so deeply flawed no one can love me, I hate myself).

I know firsthand that these are painful beliefs. I felt that climbing up the corporate ladder would help me escape the pain of being not good enough. I felt that being perfect was a good way of being because people would *need* me. My romantic relationships, when they were happening, had so little love, even though they may have seemed great from the outside. My entire life was in search of others who could make me okay. Feeling like I was not good enough kept me on the treadmill of trying to be perfect. I was in pain for years, and no matter how hard I tried, the hidden beliefs did not go away. I just felt bad.

Sound familiar? The good news is that all of this can change. It doesn't have to be that way. I changed it, and so can you.

REACTIONS AND TRIGGERS: SOUNDS LIKE A PARTY!

Emotional reactions are hard for most people to control. They seem to come out of left field. Something happens in your life that triggers a reaction, and perhaps you try your best to hold onto a shred of decorum before the people in white coats come with a straitjacket to cart your ass off to the special padded room.

It's important to know your triggers and to understand why you react as you do. The trigger is just the signal to your mind that you need to do something about an event happening outside of you (and sometimes inside of you). Reactions are tied to your deeper beliefs about the world and your place in it.

You might have spent a lifetime trying to avoid being triggered by steering clear of certain people, places, and situations (e.g., "Aunt Mary always likes to bring up the time I was five and peed the bed."). Your life can get pretty small as you try to control being triggered. You think you're looking for the best mate, employee, employer, or friend. You might believe that being in a flawless situation will let you control your triggers and reactions, so you will be happy.

It doesn't work that way. Happiness is not the absence of triggers or emotional reactions—it is the ability to exist with them. It is not kicking imperfect parts of yourself to the curb because you can't handle your emotional reaction to them. To be whole is to own all parts of yourself, and to be happy means having connections to yourself and others. And the biggest triggers come from having connections. People aren't perfect. They will trigger you.

It's pretty scary to be afraid of your own emotional reactions. In relationships, you may try hard to control the other person, so you won't be triggered. This can be exemplified in statements like, "Why don't you wear the clothes I like? I hate it when my friends see you wearing those old jeans." This keeps you emotionally barricaded and mentally keeping score, discounting or rejecting someone for every scratch and flaw. When you try to control others as a means of controlling your reactions, it comes from fear and is a means of keeping others at a distance.

It's not anyone's fault you feel the way you do. These triggers and reactions were planted a long time ago. But in the moment when you're reacting, you want it to be someone else's fault because you think it will stop the painful reaction. It might, but whatever is being triggered inside of you doesn't go away. It stays there waiting, like a zone-tailed hawk flying among the turkey vultures, ready to ambush its prey. Surprise! Out comes the crazies as you react to something you did not see coming. Your reaction to your reactions is usually one of shame, and that never feels good.

Let's say you walk into the bathroom and your partner, Larry, left your towel on the floor again. "Oh my God!" you think. Totally irritated, you lose your temper. The reaction is on autopilot and it flies under the radar of your conscious mind. You don't think, "Hey, this is an extreme reaction!" Nope, your mind is on lockdown—with blinders on. It keeps on going, flinging you into the next stage of the reaction.

Now you're pissed. What will you do?

The towel on the floor has opened up a can of worms. You are totally triggered! "How dare Larry be so disrespectful! What a jerk!" You feel different levels of conflict, along with a strong desire to strangle Larry. You cannot help how you feel: "I mean, who leaves a wet towel on the floor, especially one that doesn't belong to them? Is this a zoo? Does he hate me? Larry always does this!"

This is an example of an event that triggers a reaction that clearly has little to do with the present moment. Yes, it is your towel on the floor, but it is just a towel. Such a reaction would be way out of whack in relation to the problem. But let's say you feel you are owed, and you have been keeping a running list of the things Larry doesn't do for you. This list could be spoken or unspoken; it doesn't matter. This last inconsideration has woken up some old painful feelings. And your entire focus is consumed now by figuring out what strategy to use to finally get the point across so Larry does not do this to you anymore and you can get control of the situation and never be triggered again. You plow ahead, determined to get your way and teach Larry a lesson.

Instead, you could take a deep breath and sit down. Taking this moment to compose yourself should take the edge off a bit. Then you can ask yourself what your goal is in ignoring your old painful feelings that were triggered. It's not about the towel, and it's not about Larry. It's about you. What do you hope to accomplish in remaining in this pattern of reaction?

Here's the deal: There's a deeper reason for your reaction. It goes back to your belief system and past events in your life—moments where you felt no one heard you or cared about your feelings. Times where you did not feel important or a priority to someone who you made a priority in your life. Approach the moment with curiosity and try to be aware, so as not to be hard on yourself. Being triggered into having an emotional reaction is not the end of the world. It is an opportunity to learn about you. Changing your beliefs and patterns will require you to become aware of what is happening inside of you.

CHAPTER 3

Connecting with Yourself at the Basic Level

Before you can do any of the work in this book, you must develop an ability to connect with yourself at a basic level. This chapter will bring you to that point. It is important to really commit to the process you are about to undertake, because the more committed you are, the better your results. Please refer back to this chapter and its exercises as you proceed through the book.

LEARNING THE LANGUAGE OF EMOTIONS

Ah, emotions. Many of us are taught at a young age to get rid of them, lock them up in a jar. If you ignored them long enough, you may have thought they went away.

Emotions are a signal, a language, a clue, a connection, and so much more. Underneath almost every choice you make there is emotion, even if you are completely numb to it. In fact, decisions made from blocked emotions never end up feeling good. They just feel empty.

By the time I was a teenager, I had learned to suck down most of my emotions. If I could avoid having to interact with my parents, aside from small talk or surface things, I was okay. (I was numb.) Most of the time when I got in trouble, I remember feeling bewildered at what I was being accused of. I felt ganged up on and I could feel myself slowly shutting down. Every time I opened my mouth to offer information or an excuse, I was told I was wrong, my feelings were wrong, and I was not telling the truth.

It felt impossible in those moments to speak or feel for long. I could sense those intense feelings coming to the surface and talked myself into emotionally vacating, trying to keep a poker face just so being yelled at would be over sooner. I was protecting myself as well as I could. Sometimes the conflict escalated, because I would shut down or offer information that was not what my parents wanted to hear. I grew numb in those arguments, and outside of them too, where I tried to focus on anything but what was happening. It was uncomfortable, painful, and deeply disturbing. So, my goal was to feel none of it.

I thought I had managed well until I got older and circumstances, usually in my intimate relationships, unleashed those old feelings. I would feel I was wrong or bad, and all I wanted was to have everything return to the status quo. I had no idea what my emotions were saying. It was overwhelming, and I wanted to escape. The easiest way was to blame other people instead of connecting to my feelings. It took years for me to reconnect to my true feelings.

So, how do you learn the language of emotions? You allow yourself to connect to them, to feel them, to know them, and in turn, to pay attention to how they communicate with you. It's not the language of the mind, which is wordy, forceful, strategic, stoic, and stubborn. Emotions are a simple language, and one you knew a long time ago when you came into this world, before you fell into your childhood conditioning.

A lot of what you will find in learning this language is that it comes from learning how to feel your feelings—not *judge* your feelings, not cherry-pick the ones you like. It is a language requiring you to be open and unbiased. You will experience true connection as you learn this language and understand how you are slowly being set free from the language of the mind. Instead of being stuck in your lizard brain beliefs, you will learn to allow your emotions to be—the full range of them.

And feeling your emotions will allow you to change your lizard brain belief system. This is the most important piece of becoming friends with your emotions and learning the language they speak.

DIFFICULTY IN WORKING WITH EMOTIONS

If you have been spending your life thinking your way through your choices and your experiences, then working with your emotions might be a bit overwhelming. Part of the difficulty in working with emotions is that you are numb to so much of them. And the bigger problem with being numb or disconnected in any way emotionally is that your emotions are right where you left them. When you were busy shutting off your feelings as a small child, your emotional growth stopped. As your lizard brain was in charge of your safety, your intellect took over and left those emotions far behind. Ever wonder why many intelligent adults have temper tantrums, pout, or intellectualize others in an emotional situation, instead of expressing themselves like an adult? Now you know.

Fear is at the root of avoiding your emotions. Fear makes it difficult to acknowledge them, let alone work with them.

You may know intellectually that feelings are just a flood of chemicals yet still go to great lengths to avoid them. Keeping them bottled up leads to misery, unhealthy relationships, and even physical ailments. But reestablishing your deeper connection to yourself and your emotions will feel very freeing. Emotions can be extremely painful, true, but they won't kill you.

But, wait! You may think—and I say "think"—"I cry, I get angry, I know when I am frustrated." And I am sure you do, but that has nothing to do with this process. Remember this, your mind does not know what it feels, it just thinks. For the sake of your commitment to happiness, I am asking you to explore the concepts around emotions before you decide that you and your emotions are best friends. Instead, you may want to look at yourself and your emotions as long-lost friends about to rekindle that friendship.

What about those of you who have ice cubes where your warm and fuzzies should be, who could say, "Yeah, I have done a great job of not feeling anything for years. My emotions are under my command like a genie in a bottle. Emotions are easy if you just ignore them." You might wish this were true, but it is not. Emotions are always present, even if you have ignored them for decades.

Difficulty with emotions starts as a small child with no emotional safe haven. You may have been fearful of upsetting your parents, especially if they were critical, strict, or unpredictable. Imagine yourself as a six-year-old child, one who is really sensitive to every criticism or punishment. Your dad takes you to the auto races with his friends. You want a hot dog, but he says no. He says you can have a peanut butter and jelly sandwich. Your dad is trying to relax with his friends, so he has little patience for what you want. He goes to the food stand and comes back with the sandwich. You see it and start crying, shaking your head, saying you don't want it. Now your dad is getting pissed at you. He says you had better eat the sandwich or you will have to go to your room when you get home. You start crying more, wanting your mom. Your dad tells you to stop crying, but you can't stop your flood of feelings. You don't want to be in trouble, but you also don't want the sandwich. He finally takes the sandwich away and says if you don't stop crying, he will give you a reason to cry. He tells you that you are a spoiled brat and he's never taking you to the races again.

Meanwhile, your brain is in survival mode and panicking, trying to figure out how to stop the feelings you feel. You start thinking of how much you hate your dad, or perhaps you start fantasizing about your mom rescuing you, or you think about how sorry you are for making your dad mad. These thoughts are what you focus on, not your feelings. The feelings feel way too difficult because you have nowhere to go with them—you are stuck. You might have been called spoiled in the past and now you may believe your dad when he says you are spoiled.

This a simplistic example of how your emotions get stuck and become difficult to encounter. The point is that you have been avoiding the full breadth of your emotions for years. When emotions felt difficult as a kid, it's no surprise they can feel difficult as an adult.

LEARNING TO EMOTIONALIZE

Emotionalizing rather than intellectualizing means you put your emotions first, before your intellect, so that you build a connection to them. Emotionalizing doesn't mean you lose total control of yourself and start shouting obscenities from the rooftops. It means you have established a relationship with your emotions. It's more than an awareness of how you feel. It's knowing your motivation for your words and actions. Emotions are what the subconscious understands when it comes to having an impact on your beliefs and patterns. Your subconscious did not think a thought into becoming a belief. You felt something, which then created a negative or a positive belief in your subconscious.

I talked about your ol' lizard brain being wired for survival. It's got you focused on the "known" way of doing things. Your lizard brain is always planning, strategizing, and sizing up the situation. It only pays attention to your feelings when it comes to fear. But intellectualizing your emotional situation is never going to make you happier or less screwed up. In fact, it will make you feel more screwed up than you are.

For example: You want a relationship. A healthy, happy one. Healthy, happy relationships require emotional openness; a willingness to share your real self; intimacy, both emotional and physical; vulnerability; honesty; and most of all, love. If you are coldly logical, living in your head and deducing your latest strategy for how to get someone to fall in love with you, where is the match? Someone who is warm and open is not going to be turned on by cold and calculating. You will get rejected.

The key is to get out of your lizard brain and connect emotionally with yourself. Feeling your emotions allows you to change things at their origin, reworking your belief system at the same level your lizard brain created it.

HOW TO FEEL YOUR REAL FEELINGS

You must learn to *feel your real feelings*. You need to know the why, how, and what of those deeper feelings that you've been ignoring or shoving down. Learning to feel your feelings will help you as you work through the Eight Steps to Self-Awareness, Love, and Happiness in this book. It will help you develop self-awareness and promote emotionally inspired action, so you actually are in control of your choices, your feelings, and your happiness.

As a human being, you prefer pleasure. Part of numbing out, distracting yourself, or distancing yourself from your own emotions has to do with hoping you can just feel the positive ones and ignore those negative feelings. Unfortunately, to feel real pleasure, you have to feel the full spectrum of your emotions, which means feeling the real pain that lives there, too. It can feel pretty scary to purposefully go toward your feelings, especially if you fear that the overwhelm might take you back to an earlier time in your life, where the experiences were emotionally difficult. Remember that you are an adult now. Even if you have buried the pain with a tractor, you will still be able to live through digging it back up. Your feelings will not kill you.

What else could you fear in feeling your real feelings?

- Being out of control.
- Being stuck in your pain forever.
- Overwhelming panic that you won't able to handle it if the floodgates open.
- The possibility that people will think you're crazy.

These fears can stop you in your tracks. The unknown always sets up a pretty scary picture. The picture could be you wasting your time or being stuck in a never-ending cascade of feelings, which will turn you into someone you hate. But as you start to reconnect to your emotions and feel your feelings, you will find those fears are about as valid as the boogeyman waiting for you under your bed.

There is a difference between feeling reactive feelings at the moment and your deeper feelings. Reactive feelings include anger, frustration, blame, sadness, or fatigue, usually in response to circumstances outside of you or to a thought in your mind. The feelings you will be aiming for are much deeper. Deeper feelings are love, joy, shame, loneliness, feeling different or weird, peace, compassion, empathy, depression, distrust, and feeling in flow. Feeling in flow is a state of allowing without struggling to control things; you are quite literally in a state of being. You can feel this when you accept how you feel without forcing yourself to feel differently. A sense of ease, contentment, and connectedness stem from being in this state.

What if you decide not to feel your feelings? It will be nearly impossible to break your subconscious patterns or shift your negative beliefs. These stuffed, ignored, and distant feelings are unconsciously controlling your behavior, your actions, your words—basically, everything about you. Thinking a new thought isn't going to change them. They are the unseen motivation for what you do. So, my friend, if you want to feel good and trust yourself so you can be happy, you've gotta feel those feelings!

When I first started coaching, I asked one of my clients to feel her feelings during the day, and she could not do it. Teary-eyed, she said, "If I check in with my feelings during the day, I am afraid I will lose it." She explained how she ignored the unease in her gut, hoping it would just go away. But avoiding her feelings didn't work either, as she would end up having some sort of reactive meltdown in the privacy of her apartment.

Okay, so let's get started on how to feel your real feelings. Grab your journal and go find a quiet space. Each of the three exercises that follow takes about 10 minutes. These exercises provide you with options and a step-by-step process for how to feel your feelings. The first is a simple "body scan," which can be done at any time. The next two are techniques to use when you are in a state of reaction, either from real-world events or from purposely triggering yourself to get to the heightened state. For the third exercise, you will journal your response to help you see what is going on emotionally.

I suggest reading through all three exercises first, then coming back and doing one of the three. You will keep returning to these exercises as you go through the book. Keep in mind that language and emotion live in different parts of the brain, so this process might look a little esoteric. Keep at it; the more you do it, the easier it becomes, and you'll start to get a "feel" for it.

EXERCISE: Body Scan

This technique can be done at any time. I like doing it when I first wake up, to connect to my emotions. It's a good way to start the day and can actually shift your mood. You can also set an alarm on your phone or watch to practice scanning your body several times a day.

1. Start at the top of your head and notice everything you feel physically, from head to toe. Are your shoulders tight? Is your stomach in a knot? Does your back ache? Is there tension or heaviness anywhere? Maybe you have a generalized feeling of anxiety. Don't do anything yet, just notice.

2. Zero in on any discomfort and focus there for a minute. Be curious. Can you feel any emotions bubble up? If not, you're probably resisting out of a pattern of fear. Stick with it and see if you can connect with anything. If not, try again another morning, or when you're triggered.

3. If you do start to sense emotions brewing, allow them to surface. Don't distract yourself. Stay with the feelings until they dissipate. Ask yourself, "What does this feel like?"

4. Go deeper. Notice any flashes of pictures or scenes from your past. Do they reveal any particular fears or beliefs (fear of rejection, belief you're not good enough, etc.)? How is this currently manifesting in your life? See if you can match the fear or belief to what's going on. Maybe there's an event you're planning, a job interview, or a family dinner. Recognize that the fear or belief is less about the current event and more about the old feeling.

Whether or not you body scan, you can simply check in with yourself and your feelings throughout the day. Avoiding your emotions because you're afraid to feel what they may tell you makes anxiety and unease your daily companions. This does not help you. You know now that they will come popping out whether you want them to or not, often in ways beyond your control and in ways that shame you or make you feel guilty. So, make the time to feel them!

EXERCISE: Feel Your Real Feelings—A Technique in Reaction

Whenever you're in a heightened emotional state, usually after being triggered by someone or something outside of you, sitting with your feelings will make the discomfort dissipate more quickly. Even if you have only a few minutes to connect to yourself, it will be worth it. The first time you do this exercise, be prepared to either not feel anything or to experience an explosion of emotions you cannot get past. If you find you cannot get out of the reactive emotion, then close your eyes and breathe through it until it eases. Then, at a later time, you can revisit this.

1. As soon as you feel triggered, notice what your mind is reacting to—maybe it's a text from your partner that they have to cancel your plans for the evening.

2. Take a deep breath and close your eyes.

3. Focus on your gut or the place where you feel physical discomfort. Emotions usually manifest somewhere in the body—the stomach, chest, throat, jaw, shoulders, etc. Wherever that is, focus on it and stay there. Notice the physical sensations. Don't judge—just be with them.

4. Emotions will build and you'll start to get very uncomfortable. *Stay with it.* Your instinct will be to get up and do some dusting or make a phone call or do your taxes. (I'm serious!) This is fear trying to distract you. Don't let it. Remember, the feelings will not harm or kill you.

5. If you have never connected to your feelings, this may be far enough to go to begin with. Allow the feelings and any tears to come without judgment. Just sit and allow. That's it. Ride the emotion out until you feel lighter. To make sure you're "done," remind yourself of what triggered you (e.g., the text) and see if there's any reactivity left. If not, you've ridden the wave of emotion out and can go about your day without that heaviness. If it's still there, stay with it until it's gone.

6. If you want and have time to go deeper, stay with the sensations until your innate voice tells you what's going on. Are you getting flashes of images or scenes from your past? These flashes are windows into the root of your emotional pain. Perhaps you see yourself in a grocery store as a kid, by yourself, thinking you've been

left behind. Connecting with the source of your pain provides insight. You'll start to recognize the pattern more easily in the future and say to yourself, "This is triggering my fear of _____

_____.

I'm going to allow myself to feel these bad feelings, knowing they are about my past and not the present situation."

EXERCISE: Feeling Your Reactions

This exercise will give you more of a step-by-step method for feeling your reaction in your body. It will help you identify what is happening in real time and focus on what is going on inside. In time, you will reach the belief that is driving your behavior and will be able to do this without having been triggered into an emotional reaction.

You may feel numbness the first few times you try, but trust the process. You will get there. Before you begin be aware that once you locate the feeling in your body, notice how if you focus there you can feel your emotional feelings attached to the physical body. Just allow them to be felt. Notice the urge your brain has again to get you to distract. You may want to run, hide, or dump the feelings, but that won't make them go away. The only way to release the feelings is by connecting with them.

Now let's try it using the exercise below to fill in. You can use your journal to write your answers. An example is provided to help you with your own responses. Find a safe place where you can close your eyes and not be interrupted.

Start by getting some oxygen into your bloodstream by taking a few deep breaths. Sit back and close your eyes, then drop your focus to either your chest (heart) or stomach (solar plexus). This moves you away from the concentration of the mind and into a more intuitive place.

As you focus on your body, pay attention to the following question: "Where or whom do you feel tension with, now or in the past?" Whatever image comes up first, go with it. *Do not* question it. Just follow it as an observer rather than as the narrator you are used to being.

Now that you have a visual of a situation, locate the feeling in your body and just allow it to be felt. Notice the urge your brain has again to distract you. You may want to run, hide, or dump the feelings, but that won't make them go away. The only way to release the feelings is by connecting with them.

What are you feeling? Do you feel defensive or protective? Do you know what triggered the feeling and what the fear might be? Try not to analyze or overthink. If you just focus on the image, the picture will get clearer.

Check out the example below and then proceed to do the remainder of the exercise on your own.

Example:

- I noticed that the person I had a strong reaction to was *my mother* and he/she was acting *controlling*.

- I am seeing that I want to continue to focus on *how mad I am at her for being a jerk.*

- My pattern is to focus on *bad behavior* outside of me. My reaction to focusing on this situation outside of me is *to distract myself from how I actually feel.* I notice by focusing on my reaction and the story it creates in my mind that I *never have to get to any deeper emotion.*

- I feel it physically in my *stomach*. It feels *tight, nauseous, heavy,* making me want to *run from myself*—I don't like it. It made me feel a reaction of *being conflicted, sad, angry—short-changed and really abandoned* about myself.

- It made me feel a reaction of *exhaustion* toward the situation.

- The feeling of *being attacked and misunderstood* seems triggered by this person because it *reminds me of childhood, when I was always wrong and felt misunderstood.*

- The last time I noticed I felt this way was *last week* and what was happening at the time was *I was talking to my friend Janice and she told me she thinks I can be inconsiderate. I remember apologizing yet feeling totally misunderstood. I also thought she was a jerk in saying it to me, because she can be very inconsiderate, too.*

- What I usually do in reaction toward the other person is *defend myself* and this makes me feel *worse, like I am going down a deep dark hole.*

The triggers that I find myself reacting to are:

1. When someone accuses me of something—anything, whether I did it or not.

2. Inconsiderate family, friends, or strangers.

3. Being misunderstood.

4. When someone blames me for something they did—no responsibility!

5. When someone doesn't know what they are talking about and they are criticizing someone else.

Now fill in the blanks yourself, using your journal:

I noticed that the person I had a strong reaction to was

_____

and he/she was acting _____

_____.

I am seeing that I want to continue to focus on _____

_____.

My pattern is to focus on _____

_____

outside of me. My reaction to focusing on this situation outside of me

is _____

_____.

I notice by focusing on my reaction and the story it creates in my

mind that I _____

_____.

Now, focus on finding the feeling in your body. If you are struggling, you can go back to the beginning of this exercise and start again. If you are able to shift your focus to feeling your bodily sensations, then you can proceed to the next statement.

I feel it physically in my (body location) _____

_____.

It feels _____,

making me want to _____

_____.

I feel _____

about myself—I don't like it. It made me feel a reaction of_____

_____

about myself.

It made me feel a reaction of _____

_____ toward the situation.

The feeling of _____ seems triggered by this person

because it _____

_____.

The last time I noticed I felt this way was _____,

and what was happening at the time was _____

_____.

What I usually do in reaction toward the other person is _____

_____

and this makes me feel _____

_____.

The triggers that I find myself reacting to are:

1. _____

2. _____

3. _____

4. _____

5. _____

The feelings in your body may be tumultuous for a while, but the goal is to get deeper in feeling, past the tumult. For now, just make a connection. Once you know the triggers and you feel the feeling inside of you, you've made that connection! Your reaction is the starting point.

BUILD THAT SELF-AWARENESS MUSCLE

To master self-awareness is to find yourself; to be the observer of yourself in words, actions, thoughts, and feelings; to inhabit your body fully; and to be emotionally present as much as possible in your life instead of fighting it. Knowing your triggers and what causes you to react is a major step into awareness of yourself.

You go to the gym to build physical muscle. Where do you go to build self-awareness muscle? *You!* To be clear on who you are, why you do what you do, think what you think, believe what you believe, know what you know, and feel what you feel, take full responsibility for yourself and understand at a deeper level that you are the cause and creator of your life.

Building self-awareness can be as simple as the following: Imagine being at lunch with your work friends. You are all drinking margaritas. What does the margarita taste like? How does it feel as you drink it? What do you notice about the experience of drinking it? Now, what about the social aspect of the lunch? What are you talking about? How do you feel? Are you being genuine, or trying to impress? Why? Because you feel connected and excited? Or is it so you will belong or seem smart or can lead the conversation? See, all the questions here are not to interrogate yourself but to ask with curiosity and compassion, to "know thyself." Grasping the *why* lets you see what is really going on with you. The deeper the why, the better the understanding.

Self-awareness can grow every moment of every day. As I sit here typing, how do I feel? I feel into my body and I notice I feel a bit uptight. The first connection I make to feeling uptight is that I need to go to the grocery store and might not have time. Feelings come up and pass. All of this is to say, I am aware of what is going on with me at any point in time.

Notice what pisses you off in someone else. What don't you like in your friend who always cancels? Perhaps they remind you of something you find problematic in yourself. For self-awareness, use the situation for your own growth. Look at your own inconsistencies. I guarantee you have them. Find them and own them. The awareness you gain is worth it.

Be aware of how you feel when you are frustrated about something. Try to recall a time you complained about a partner or friend. If you paid attention to your body as you were complaining, you might have noticed feeling unrest inside. You may have found a matching internal voice that was judging you as you complained. Dig deeper to find what you avoid dealing with in yourself—this grows your self-awareness.

Self-awareness grows with taking accountability for what you say, think, and do. In my work, people talk about breaking up all the time. When someone cannot decide whether to stay with their partner or go, they are stuck. Without self-awareness, they mentally go back and forth, adding up a list of problems stemming from their partner's behavior. There is no ownership of why they chose to be with this person, nor of their own contribution to the relationship. Without awareness, they just leave, seeking relief, still not knowing their real motivation. They move on physically, but not emotionally. The next relationship has the same issues, including focusing on the other person as the problem—no growth or happiness there.

Situations of great distress are tremendous opportunities for taking responsibility and growing your self-awareness. Embrace them! The deeper you go and the more you see yourself without your lizard brain sunglasses on, the better you can make choices for your happiness.

WATCH OUT FOR RESISTANCE TO CHANGE

The amount of stress you experience is determined by how much energy you expend resisting. You can resist facing events, moments, and feelings. The same goes for resisting change. No matter what you resist, it comes from the fear of being out of control emotionally. The roots of this live in your belief system. It stems from your negative/fearful beliefs. These beliefs set your perceptions. So you avoid negative feelings by trying to talk yourself out of them, telling yourself another story, finding distraction, assigning blame, and so on. If you look at almost any choice you resist, it's because of fear of the emotional impact of the situation.

Resistance is stressful because even if you want to change, your subconscious sees change as a threat. And the truth is that resisting something still doesn't give you any control. Unwanted change happens anyway, or you stay mired in circumstances you can't stand.

Resist experience → Resist present moment → Resist life → Resist change → Stress

The more you resist your circumstances, the more stress you bring into your life. If you resist everything, your life fills with stress. Wherever you look, there is stress and conflict. You do not like your job. You do not like your family. You do not like your classmates. You do not like yourself. Nothing that you see or encounter meets your approval and *you won't change it*. It feels too hard and too scary. It may feel like a big ball of yarn that you cannot untangle. It is guaranteed to produce emotionally dysfunctional situations. If you resist these experiences, you add yet more stress to your life, and your emotional issues become more intense. Your body is telling you, through your feelings, to deal, rather than resist.

For instance, you can be resistant to the experience of changing your job. Even though you hate your job and avoid or delay doing what your boss asks you to do, you fear change more than you hate your job. You ain't going nowhere. You might hope for some kind of miracle where everyone else changes. It's too overwhelming for you to change, as you're consumed by "what if" thoughts about the future.

When you have a pattern of resistance, it can be difficult to change it. Take the example of Carmen, who decided to quit her job after 10 years to start her own business. She had saved up enough money to exist for one year without having to take another job. Her parents had always worked nine to five. Her mom was worried and was not supportive of Carmen quitting and doing her own thing. For Carmen, this business was a long time coming, something she had dreamed about. At the same time, she found ways to make the change difficult. Six months after quitting her job, she kept putting off the extra training she needed for her business. She also dragged her feet with actually starting her business. She already had a location and was paying rent, but had not started the design or construction of the space. She could not figure out what she was afraid of, besides failure. Her excuses ranged from needing to do more research to waiting for other people to step in and help; these thoughts kept her focused on being pissed off at them instead of mad at herself.

In reality, the only one holding Carmen back was Carmen. She feared not only failure, but also success. This fear of how the business could change her life made her resist her own choice. She was also stressed out! We worked on the practical aspects of accountability, but we also took a deep dive into the fears Carmen had around success, around being different and trusting herself. As we worked on these beliefs and others, Carmen started making headway and feeling a ton better.

When you do not like what is happening and you resist it as well as doing anything about it, you have to look at what feelings are driving the behavior. What you fear will try to stop you from moving forward into the unknown. Resistance can show up as self-sabotage, martyrdom, defiance, venting/gossiping about the same situation, holding on to dysfunction, rebelling, and not doing what you really want. It always stands in the way of your happiness as you fight to stay right where you are—even when you're miserable.

Deciding to remain in resistance means you will continue to look at life through a series of confirmation biases, meaning you will interpret new information as evidence that your negative beliefs are true, so you won't change. It's a pretty fearful and stressful way to live.

What do you do if you are in the act of resistance? You guessed it: feel your feelings.

Knowing what resistance feels like physically can help you to find those feelings. Resisting physically feels like walls inside of you—heaviness and tightness (even pain) in your body. Don't struggle against the feelings. If you insist on struggling, you will get in an argument with yourself, back and forth in your own head, going nowhere. Instead, feel the physical sensations. What does your body feel like, and what is it trying to tell you? The feelings are what make you resistant, not the thoughts.

Now that you have had some practice feeling your feelings, you are ready to embark on the Eight Steps to Self-Awareness, Love, and Happiness. You can do them in any order and return to this chapter any time you need a reminder on how to feel your feelings. Each step explores behaviors that make you unhappy. You will learn how to unearth your motivations for doing what you do, tracing back the negative beliefs you learned from your lizard brain, many of which stem from insecure attachment and the influence of the drama triangle.

As you read your way through his book you will start to understand how you create your own problems, and knowing this will lead you toward how to solve them. You will unlearn old patterns and replace them with new ones. You will become happier.

CHAPTER 4

Step 1—Stop Avoiding Your Fears and Attaching to Outcomes

Because perfectionists fear feeling their emotions, especially negative emotions like fear, they are compelled to control outcomes. They think that controlling outcomes will relieve their anxiety, but it doesn't. In essence, what they try to avoid, they end up experiencing anyway.

The solution is to stop avoiding fear by feeling your way through an emotional reaction and surrendering to how you feel, letting go of prescribed outcomes in the process.

FEAR IS A BASTARD

You have probably heard the advice from a commercial more than once: "Feel the fear and just do it!" Doesn't this make it sound like coming out alive from a parachute jump would be a cure-all for fear? When I successfully ran a 26.2-mile marathon that had me terrified, all my friends told me, "You can do anything now!" But that win made no impact on what I could achieve in my personal relationships and life. Pushing through the emotion of fear by taking on physical challenges can't teach anyone how to be more emotionally intimate with themselves or with another person. Unless there is a relatable emotional component to the physical challenge, forget about it changing you at your core. To change at your core requires awareness of what your own emotional fears are and a willingness to feel them by staying with them—not pushing through with the mind or going around them. Deep change like this also requires the courage to look at what's on the other side of the protective wall that your fears have built up around the real you.

Good old lizard brain served us well when we still lived in caves and faced real dangers. But in modern society, where we no longer need to worry about being attacked by wild animals outside our front door, lizard brain still means to protect us from harm.

The things we fear may be abstract or concrete: loss of closeness, stature, love, a job, how others view us, relationships, material things, and so on. Our brains, unfortunately, don't know the difference between fear brought on by true physical danger and fear brought on by a scary thought or emotion. The trigger mechanism in the brain is the same, and the physiological intensity of the reaction is the same.

Fear is a buzzkill! It will sabotage your curiosity, your courage, your happiness, and your peace of mind. It will limit your capacity to experience life and your relationships in all their richness. It's not that you have to (or even can) get rid of fear altogether—it's wired into us—it is just that you don't have to give fear the license to take over the steering wheel of your life. You can just pick its ass up and move it over to the passenger seat, then take the wheel. This will take commitment and practice, but at some point and in certain situations, you'll be able to kick fear right out of the car and onto the curb.

However, if you do so without understanding what your personal fears are, they will jump right back into the car with you at the first opportunity, even if you just climbed Mount Everest or ran that marathon you didn't think you could do. Ever notice how your good feelings of success go *poof* pretty quickly and you find yourself right back to feeling like your old, conditioned self?

UNDERSTAND THE MANY SIGNPOSTS OF FEAR

Fear is like a box of Cracker Jack: you never know what's at the bottom of the box. It has many ways of keeping things the same, so you stay in your familiar zone. But there are signposts that give you clues. Here are some of them:

- Experiencing physical sensations such as heaviness
- Trying to take impossible circumstances under control when it is out of your control
- Avoiding or dragging yourself to things you would normally enjoy
- Coming up with a million excuses about why you can't do something
- Having anxiety but no clarity as to why

- Clinging to others or to a relationship that is over
- Waking up exhausted, even when you've slept enough
- Saying you want something and then running from it
- Having pity parties because you feel sorry for yourself
- Needing the outcome that you think is the only way for you to be okay
- Being angry or picking a fight
- Distancing emotionally and perhaps physically from others
- Numbing out with food, work, and other substances
- Lying and telling stories, to yourself and others
- Blaming others and outside circumstances
- Being guarded and suspicious, not trusting
- Being disconnected from people and from life in general
- Not dealing with reality as it is, avoiding disappointment through escapism

These are common patterns for coping with fear, and they are easy to spot. They are both strategies and signposts, and they keep you in fear. You'll find that once you start to really pay attention, you will see that they are trying to help you by protecting you from your greatest fears coming true.

I used to throw myself pity parties. When I got divorced, I wanted freedom, but I did not know what true freedom felt like. Suddenly I was free of my husband, but I was terrified of being alone and of life, so I circled the wagons around me and shut down my life. I felt sorry for myself and my inability to create the amazing life I had imagined—fear ruled me. I already felt like a failure with my divorce, and I believed I was not a good person, so how could I deserve that amazing life I had imagined? I felt lonely, tired, and fearful of going out to do things on my own when my kids were with their dad. I had no idea why. I focused most of my attention on working and on my kids. Even though I felt awful, there was a comforting familiarity to it.

It took years, but I worked through my fear to a point where I was no longer wallowing in sorrow over my life not looking how I had imagined. My pity parties lessened as I started to free myself from the prison of my fear-based beliefs. I did this by feeling my fears. I started to change when I began to take risks emotionally, exploring my fears instead of avoiding or ignoring them.

FEAR-BASED BELIEFS

Our fears go wherever we go. They also come packaged in fear-based beliefs that ol' lizard brain catalogs for us so it knows when to throw up that No Trespassing! sign. One fear-based belief that drove me in my relationships was ending up alone. It kept me from being vulnerable, emotionally intimate, and real in my communication, and from taking responsibility for my words and actions. I was always walking on eggshells, not wanting to screw anything up. I wanted to stick with what I knew so as not to risk losing anyone. Being vulnerable or emotionally intimate made me too anxious. Each time I went there, my fear-based belief warned me subconsciously that if I dared to try those things, I would definitely end up alone. And so, I would continue on eggshells, not opening myself up. To my chagrin, the prophecy kept coming true! I kept ending up alone.

If you avoid reaching down to the level of the beliefs ol' lizard brain is operating from, you won't be able to try any new, emotionally risky behavior. Treating your fears like the enemy, or avoiding them like smallpox at Christmas, only means they will keep driving you and your choices.

Every single one of us carries fear-based beliefs. Here are some of the most common. As you read this list, use what you learned in Chapter 3 and pay attention to how you feel.

- There is no real solution to the pain I feel.
- I might be a failure.
- I have no value—I am insignificant.
- Things are out of control, and I won't be able to cope.
- I might be found out as a fake or a phony.
- I can't appear weak or needy.
- I will be abandoned.
- I will be swallowed up by someone else's emotions and lose myself in their drama.
- I will be swallowed up by my own emotions and lose myself in my own drama.
- I might choose wrong, and the consequences will be horrible.
- I will end up alone for the rest of my life.
- I will be proven deeply unlovable.
- I will be left with nothing or nobody if I let go.
- I will get what I think I want, and I won't like it.
- Gosh, without my fears, who would I be?

Do any of these fears ring a bell for you? Are you able to feel them in your physical body? If not, if you can think about these fears without a physiological response, that is evidence of a pattern of avoiding your feelings.

Now stop for a moment, right now, and think of a situation that triggers the fear-based belief you most identified with in the list—or anything that scares you. Go into your body. I bet you will feel something physical now, maybe like the sensation you get when the rollercoaster is headed downward and your stomach has dropped to your feet. Or maybe your throat is tightening. Perhaps your chest feels constricted or heavy, or your stomach feels like hurling. Or you feel suddenly like you are moving through cement. The physical sensation can be a sudden backache or a headache, too; your legs could feel glued to the floor, or you might feel like running or doing a high jump!

Now sit still with the physical sensations. That is scary in and of itself, right? Can you see how this trepidation of feeling fear would keep you stuck and make you want to put a muzzle on it, fast? Those sensations are what make us want to run the other way and avoid our fears. In fact, they make us want to control the very circumstances that would bring us anywhere near feeling like that.

EPIGENETICS IS ALL ABOUT INFLUENCE!

In Chapter 2, I told you that fear-based beliefs lock into place during childhood. But the real kick in the pants is that the majority of our fearful beliefs come down through the generations to us. Have you heard about epigenetics? It's what controls or determines what your genes do, and you influence your genes by what you do. Everything from what you eat to how you sleep—it all impacts your genes. The good news is that the way they are impacted is reversible, so you have a form of control over your genes. And when it comes to what you inherited, it can change—the programming we inherit from our ancestors' lives is not static.

Let's say some ancestor of yours, way before you were born, decided to go for a swim after eating lunch. He drowned. Other family members figured he drowned because he swam on a full stomach, even though the cause of death could have been a heart attack or something else. The experience imprinted many people with the lizard brain rule that you can expect to die if you swim on a full stomach. The rule got passed down to you. Now every time you think about swimming after a meal, you go into a panic without knowing why.

Stories like this make up the majority of fear-based beliefs, whether passed down or in present time, and we are clueless about most of them. We may never get to know them, but we can do something about changing how we relate to the fear response.

Let's say you are the rule-breaker in your family and you now understand that there is probably some story behind the panic you experience each time you go swimming after eating a meal. You decide you want to change the story. After eating at a buffet, you gently let yourself into the pool even as panic floods your body. You stay with the sensations as you swim around in the pool. Miraculously, you live! You let yourself feel amazing about it and the fear melts away into the water. It shifts to joy and gratitude. At that moment you've created a new story in your emotional space, a story that your lizard brain will be only too happy to make into a new belief: it's safe to swim after you eat! And right there, you've exponentially expanded your capacity to experience life. Had you jumped into the pool while ignoring or pushing past the panic rather than staying with it, you wouldn't have accomplished this.

NOT LIKING FEAR DOESN'T MAKE IT GO AWAY!

Fear and fear-based beliefs don't go away just because you become good at avoiding circumstances that might trigger them. Fear is sneaky that way. You can have it all under control, looking like you are flawlessly happy and on top of your game, then someone says or does something, or a situation happens that triggers you, and the whole charade comes crashing down. Basically, you're avoiding your fears. You can only be happy as long as life cooperates with your master plan. As soon as things don't go your way, you go back to feeling awful in the span of seconds. No matter how hard you try to avoid anything that could emotionally light your fear on fire, it will always happen sooner or later. Life does life.

Wishing your fear away, hiding from it, or pretending it doesn't exist makes no emotional impact on your subconscious. It's like repeating a list of one hundred affirmations—they are just words you say. Repeating affirmations such as "I am abundant" in the hope that it will change your fearful beliefs, when you are actually afraid to spend money on necessities, doesn't work. It's akin to blowing up a balloon with a hole in it—you can keep on trying, but you get nowhere.

If you think you're happiest when avoiding fear, think again. It takes a lot of energy and hard work to keep every inch of our lives under control, to have our way. Ever find yourself in a state of inertia, like you're walking through cement, just at the thought of sharing how you really like this new person and not knowing if it will be reciprocated? What about when you distract yourself from writing your blog, because TV is so much more interesting? Or when you numb your true feelings in a discussion with your partner so you can seem to come across better and feel intellectually superior to them? All of this numbing, abstracting, and pretending takes energy away from the authentic you. Being disconnected from yourself is not genuine, lasting happiness. Not feeling the full spectrum of your feelings, including your fears, limits your capacity to enjoy and be enriched by life.

STRATEGIES TO AVOID FEAR ADD UP TO ZERO

Over the years, we develop many strategies to avoid our fears. These strategies give us an illusion of having control over our lives. For example, when we criticize or judge others, we're often avoiding our fears by making someone else the focus. We might even claim we are being emotionally expressive and helpful when we point out to people in our lives what they could do to improve themselves or their behavior. But if it sounds anything like the following, then we are just verbalizing how out of control and victimized we feel: "Why me?"; "You don't listen! I keep explaining and you're just not understanding me!"; "This just feels like too much work"; "Are you an idiot, or what?"; and "When will people get a clue and see what I see?"

Another fear-avoidance strategy is believing "I yam what I yam," that's just the way things are, while simultaneously hoping your circumstances will change.

Take the situation of Mark, who liked Anna. They had been going out for a few weeks. Anna was totally frustrated, because Mark did not like to text or call between dates. The only time he would do either was to confirm their meeting. Anna felt a lag in getting to know Mark and felt stuck and frustrated. She raised the issue with him, but he wasn't interested in compromising, although he liked Anna. He felt she needed to understand that he was just that way. He was comfortable being emotionally unavailable and keeping people at a distance. It worked for Mark because he was afraid to get too close—it felt too messy. Even though Anna enjoyed seeing Mark, she grew tired of doing it only on his terms, with no real progression to their relationship. So, she chose to stop seeing him. He was upset and blamed Anna, saying she should have been more patient and less needy.

With this strategy of blaming circumstances or other people every time life doesn't cooperate and the scary feelings come up, you have an out. For example, a woman looking to leave a verbally abusive partner might say, "I can't leave him because the kids and I cannot afford to live on our own. I guess I could look for a promotion or get a better paying job, but my job is easy, and I am lazy."

SELF-CARE MOMENT

Whenever you find yourself claiming, "I yam what I yam," and it is based in a fear, ask yourself why you have this fear and see if you can take a step toward being real. For example, saying "I have a fear of getting close to you, so I avoid talking to you between our dates" is more authentic.

Insisting on your way is the biggest fear-avoidance strategy of all, and it's the most delusional of them because there is really no way to control people or circumstances forever. Sure, you might pull off having the people in your life cooperate with your master plan for a little while. You may even believe you're doing the right thing by deciding on outcomes you think are the best for everyone involved. But the people you are trying to control will not want to stay under your control for very long, however charming and nice you are about it.

A very subtle way of having your way is hiding out. This strategy provides a foolproof escape-hatch option to all those messy fear sensations getting unleashed. Brenda, one of my clients, hid out in plain sight in conversations. Whenever she felt uneasy about where she stood with a person, especially her fiancé's sister, Petunia, Brenda's strategy was, "Let's talk about what you want." She liked to lose herself in the conversation between them, on Petunia's terms. If Petunia wanted to talk about the hair on a bug's back, Brenda found herself engaging with the topic, even though she had no interest in hairs on the backs of bugs. She wanted Petunia to like and even love her. The stakes seemed high because if Petunia didn't like her, Brenda felt that she might lose the relationship with her fiancé. She feared losing the relationship with her fiancé because she assumed his sister had a great deal of influence over him. By talking about whatever made Petunia happy, Brenda thought rejection and potential loss were in the rearview mirror. She'd feel a sense of relief wash over her whenever she let Petunia direct their conversations.

But she worked so hard to accommodate Petunia that she had absolutely no idea what her fiancé's sister actually thought or felt about her. She couldn't be sure Petunia would not reject her, and that thought kept her in a state of unease. She was not solving her fear by swallowing it and pretending; it still lurked inside of her. In the end, how much was she really getting her way in keeping her relationship with Petunia's brother safe?

THE GOBLIN WE ALL FEAR: DISAPPOINTMENT

Disappointment can feel like your whole world is crashing down around you, all the more so if you have been trying to keep tight control over circumstances. Look at it this way: if you've been working hard to have your way and despite your best effort things fall apart, then it's a short hop and skip to feeling like you're a failure. But wait! Even if disappointment does happen, you can still blame outer circumstances or hold out hope that something will change in your favor. The only time I recommend having hope is in a life-or-death situation, like hanging off a cliff by your fingernails. Otherwise, hoping for change without doing the work of changing is a dead end.

Not dealing with disappointment takes many forms. For example, let's say your husband lost his "secure" job. You feared this would happen and then it happened. You still harbor some fear-based beliefs from when your dad kept losing jobs when you were a kid. Your stomach wraps up in knots every time you remember the many difficult changes that came with each loss. Because you fear the worst, you kick into action: you help your husband with his résumé, send him job listings he can apply to online, and give him positive affirmations and books to read on how to find another job. At the same time, you start to worry he is not trying hard enough, so you begin to pressure him and criticize his lack of effort. He is not meeting your expectations! You're desperately fighting off disappointment, and your anxiety mounts by the day. No, thank you disappointment—you aren't wanted here!

But to keep your fearful feelings at bay, you need your husband's full cooperation. He does not seem to be on the same page. Now you find yourself growing disappointed in him, and the marriage starts to feel like there is a wedge in it.

If you were to feel your fearful feelings instead of acting out, you might find yourself able to self-soothe by getting deeper to your core belief around scarcity or loss. Instead of running from disappointment by trying to fix the situation, you would feel it, and it would pass through.

You might look at his job loss as an opportunity for you both to go in a new direction. You might then take emotionally inspired action and go in a direction that seems scary. Paradoxically, this would lessen fear's grip on you. You could then talk to your husband about your feelings, without blame. Perhaps he could share as well. It would bring you closer.

Avoiding disappointment is as dangerous to our ultimate happiness as avoiding fear. All disappointment is based in fearing your authentic feelings around loss. Instead of dealing with your disappointment, you become anxious, confused, out of control, depressed, angry, sad, and even more afraid. Your familiar strategies kick in.

Here are some examples of how people avoid disappointment:

- If I lose the game, I will feel *awful.* Better to feign illness or noninterest and avoid disappointment.

- If I ask him/her out on a date, I could be *rejected.* I'd feel very *disappointed.* Guess I will not ask him/her out.

- If I start my business with my life savings, and it fails, I will feel *like a loser,* so I'd better not risk it. I'll stay with the paycheck.

- If I break up with him/her, I will *feel lonely and isolated,* so I'd better stay here, where I know I won't be alone.

- I need to invest in those stocks because they are proven winners. But if I were to lose money, I would feel *irresponsible and embarrassed.* The shame and disappointment would be rough, so I will keep my money in bonds.

The point is that the negative feelings around disappointment can be as strong as those around fear, and your lizard brain will want to save you from experiencing them. It will turn the situation into something else—making you ignore the options or carry false hope, distracting you with something else. A common default strategy is to blame someone else, saying, "She told me to do it! If I hadn't listened to her, none of this would have happened." Or, "He is the one who picked out the house. It's his fault it's a money pit and now we're broke."

Conversely, when someone is blaming you for their disappointment, what do you do to avoid it? Do you defend yourself, argue, or find fault with them? The next exercise will help you get clear on why you may avoid disappointing someone. It will show you how to take action and handle it even if you inevitably disappoint them.

The bottom line is that the lizard brain just doesn't want to feel bad, no matter what, and you go with lizard brain as if on autopilot.

EXERCISE: Experiencing Disappointment

Okay, let's run through a situation where you fear causing disappointment in someone else. This will take 20 to 30 minutes. Grab your journal and find a quiet space.

Think of a situation where you are avoiding disappointing someone.

1. What is the situation? (Example: You are avoiding breaking up with someone you do not feel a connection to anymore.)

2. How important is it to control their response to you? (Very. I need him/her to still think I am good person.)

3. What fear-based belief are you afraid will be confirmed if you disappoint this person? (Example: They will tell me that I'm a loser and a jerk, which confirms I'm not a good person.)

4. How will you feel if you keep things the same? What is the cost? (I will feel like coming out of my skin. I'll complain, feel tense, anxious, and stuck. I will be pretending, and that feels horrible. The cost is my well-being.)

5. Worst-case scenario: Now imagine taking the risk of being honest, even if the person you fear disappointing stirs up a huge emotional storm in your direction. Dig deep. How does it feel? Can you take responsibility for your choice, be compassionate, and not defend yourself?

6. Can you see where you can take the risk to grow yourself and actually set another person free from an inauthentic situation? (I believe that if I break up with them they can be with someone they connect with, instead of being tolerated. I will feel better about myself and trust myself more to make a fair and honest choice.)

Having expectations in life inevitably leads to disappointment. You will mentally strategize your emotions to control your reactions to others, to control if or when you do something, to control how you are seen/perceived, to control everything that could possibly trigger the pain inside of you—all to steer clear of disappointment. But having expectations that require you to try to control the outcome is painful and tiresome. Look at all this work! This does not lead to true happiness. True happiness comes when you let things be what they are—even disappointment—and take responsibility by feeling the feelings you have around them.

NOW STOP AVOIDING YOUR FEARS AND ATTACHING TO OUTCOMES

How in the hell do you stop avoiding your fears and attaching to specific outcomes you swore you needed to be happy? Well, you really need to meet your fear where it lives: in your emotional body. You need to learn to feel your fear or disappointment in the situation itself, not in your head. You need to become aware of what your unique fear-based patterns are and reeducate your lizard brain.

If you look at fear or disappointment objectively, you can see that they are feelings, not a death sentence. You can tell yourself not to make it into a bigger deal than it is and quit all the strategies you've become aware you use to avoid feeling bad.

By choosing to turn toward fear rather than avoid it, you will find that the fear you thought was your greatest foe is actually your greatest friend and the key to your authentic well-being. You are alive; the unpleasantness will pass. Let the fear and its buddy, disappointment, run through you and see what choices await you on the other side. Give up your strategies! They're not the last coconuts on the island.

Stepping into the gray area where you are not controlling the outcome of a situation will be scary. The first few times you try this you may feel anxious and ungrounded. You might fear that you'll spin out of control. It might even feel like an out-of-body experience!

You can relax. Really. Even if your lizard brain is going a million miles an hour, showing you every fear you (or your ancestors) ever had coming true, it will usually be in a very hazy way. Remember, your lizard brain is concerned only with keeping you safe and alive, based on what seemed to have worked in the past. It's not concerned with your happiness. Also remember that you can retrain it over time.

First, you have to know there are stories behind your fear-based beliefs that have little to do with what is happening to you now. Then, keep yourself from grabbing onto the familiar strategies you've used to save you from your negative feelings. Finally, let the physiology of the feelings run through you and ride them until they have passed. They do pass. Before they pass, you can dig deeper and get to the root of what is driving you to do what you are doing when you are reacting to fear.

The more you do this process, the easier it is to do and the faster the feelings will pass through you. The lizard brain retrains each time. Next thing you know, you have become the master of your life. Ironically, you have gotten there by giving up control, seeking deeper connection with yourself, and letting your feelings be what they are.

EXERCISE: Breaking Fear's Grip

This exercise can be done with any fear you have.

Grab your journal, set aside about 30 minutes, and find a quiet, comfortable place where you won't be interrupted and can close your eyes. Remember the exercises in Chapter 3 on how to feel your feelings. It's the physical sensations in your body that you must follow when you answer these questions, not the chattering in your mind. When you are asked to look back, for example, don't do it mentally. Remain emotionally open to whatever answers, images, or sensations come up for you. Take a moment to notice and appreciate what your emotional place can reveal to you about your fears.

> Breaking fear's grip takes courage and commitment. Courage, because you will be uncomfortable, and courage that makes it possible for you to take a risk. Commitment, because you must be willing to try something totally outside your familiar universe.

Overcoming Insecure Attachment

Reflect on the following questions and write your answers down.

1. What early painful life experience made you vow that you would *never* do the same thing you witnessed your parents do? Why did this event cause you pain? What fear did it create in you? When you made this vow, what strategy (or strategies) did you decide would be the best way to avoid ending up like them?

2. Did your strategy (or strategies) actually work in preventing the same experience from happening in your life? Were you able to avoid pain and disappointment, or did you end up doing things the same way your parents did? If you ended up doing the same things, how does it repeat itself now? And does it make you more afraid of it happening again?

3. How has using these strategies to avoid fear benefited you? There is always a benefit.

4. What is one step you could take right now, that would feel risky, toward stopping this old strategy of avoiding what you fear and allowing yourself to feel your feelings of fear? An example would be that when you have an argument with your partner, you usually shut down, pout, and ignore them. The risk would be to get close—to be vulnerable, remember you love them, and be open to a resolution. What does it feel like to imagine doing this risky behavior?

Taking an emotionally risky choice means that *you will neither plan nor decide on the outcome before you take the risky action*. If you know or plan the outcome, it's not risky. Just letting go of an outcome and acting is a risk in and of itself. Holding onto an outcome will cause you anxiety, because you will need your action to be met with your preferred reaction. Whatever you hold onto will keep you stuck in the same controlling behavior. Here's an example:

Emotionally risky action: "I am going to take an emotionally risky action by calling my parents after not speaking for the past couple of years. I have no idea what will happen, but I need to be compassionate and express my true feelings to them no matter what happens."

Not emotionally risky action: "I want to take an emotionally risky action by calling my parents after not speaking for the past couple of years, but I need to guarantee they will not reject me. If they reject me, then what is the point of the action?"

To be as authentic as possible means not holding onto an outcome when you commit to taking a risk, as you can see from the example. Being aware of why you are taking a risk and then allowing yourself to feel however you feel (there is no right or wrong way to feel), without trying to force yourself to have a specific "positive" feeling, will also impact how you change yourself through your risk. And finally, if you don't honor your feelings, who will? Let's go back to the example above:

> I was afraid, and my chest was tight as I dialed my parents. It was scary. They might not answer, or they might reject me. I just needed to say what is true for me. "Hi, Mom and Dad, it's been a long time. I am just calling to let you know that I love you and miss you."

There is no way to analyze risk when it comes to your emotions. To analyze involves letting the mental aspect take over, trying to measure costs and benefits. This is both impossible and futile. You cannot analyze, weigh, or consider all the possible results from taking a risk. Every time you analyze before taking an emotional risk, you will find an excuse not to take it. Your fear of an unhappy ending scares you more than the possibility of freeing yourself of the fear.

You must make the jump and trust that you will be okay. Even if you go through pain or discomfort, you will survive and then thrive.

What else can you do to stop being driven by your unacknowledged fears?

- Surrender to your fear-based beliefs—don't fight them. Accept that they exist. You developed them based on the models in your environment, and you created patterns to support them. Fighting them is a distraction, which drains you of energy and works against you. To continue to fight keeps you stuck in the negative behaviors outlined in this book.

- Open up your perception of life. Look for evidence that the opposite of your beliefs is true. If you think someone is a jerk—look for where they are kind. If you think *you're* a jerk, see where you are kind. In a bad relationship, see where you've pigeonholed your partner into being wrong, and accept where they might be right. See what else is true that you normally see from a place of fear and be open to what you normally categorize as wrong, bad, or a problem.

- Look in the mirror whenever you see yourself trying to control an outcome. Feel your feelings and ask: What is the fear you are trying to avoid, and what will happen if things don't go your way? Will you be okay? Yes, you will!

- Let go of believing you have any control over someone else or over a situation. You don't. Even with force, people don't change because you want them to. They change when they want to. Every time you find yourself needing someone to do what you want, stop yourself, breathe, and surrender. One of the most freeing things you can do is be honest with them. Don't let fear keep the lies coming—tell them what you were trying to do.

- Step into making changes slowly. The process will work for you in a much kinder way.

Fear is the opposite of freedom. Freedom starts within you. The more you let go of the limiting beliefs, people, and situations you hold tight to through fear, the clearer it becomes that fear is an illusion. It skews your relationship to everything in your life.

In seeing what happens when you let go and no longer attach to outcomes, you begin to understand at a core level how life works and find your place in it. Stopping the struggle of fear becomes one of the most monumental steps you can take toward thriving.

CHAPTER 5

Step 2—Stop Trying to Be Perfect

Perfectionists hide their true selves in order to present a perfect self to the world. They avoid criticism and negative attention and seek success and validation by getting exactly what they think they want. Fear of doing something wrong keeps them on their toes. This pattern is a house of cards, so when things are less than perfect, perfectionists go over the edge emotionally.

Because perfectionism is such a restricting way to live and view the world, the solution is openness, transparency, and vulnerability, while learning to face the fear of loss and replace this fear with self-love.

HOW PERFECTIONISM LEADS TO UNHAPPINESS

You may not see yourself as a perfectionist, or perhaps you believe being a perfectionist is an awesome position to take in your life. Being a perfectionist is not a positive character attribute. It is the need to avoid failure at all costs. For some, it is a daily, abstract goal, which is impossible to achieve and sustain because of its intangible nature. It is a moving target, with your hard effort aimed at receiving some kind of validation or approval. But even more importantly, it has you working your ass off to avoid disapproval. This is a difficult, exhausting, and negative way to live, because perfection is usually unattainable for ordinary humans.

It's all about the world of validation. If you can pull a snake out of your hat, tame it by blowing a whistle, and put it back in its cage without getting bit, you're pretty damn amazing! Did it impress the world? How long did the feeling of accomplishment last?

Perfectionism is stressful. Not only are you holding yourself account-able to very high expectations, but you also hold the rest of the world there. It's not like Disneyland. I mean, what happens when someone lets you down at work by turning a project in late? Or your date cancels at the last minute? Or your boyfriend didn't do what you wanted to do for Valentine's Day? He knew what you wanted! But did he do it? Nope! Something simple, like waking up in the morning with an expectation that your day will go well, and instead stumbling from one issue to another leaves you feeling pissed and disappointed. These expectations, and what you have wrapped up in them, will rob you of any possible happiness.

In holding yourself up to a very high standard, how often do you feel good? Are your efforts aimed toward the goal of happiness or toward the goal of impressing others and dodging criticism? What about when mistakes and failures happen? How does that feel?

For a perfectionist, it feels bad. Even the thought of it can have you breaking out in hives. Being a perfectionist, believing that you will someday be rewarded for living this way, equals a sum of zero in the happiness equation. You will never reach this imaginary plateau.

PERFECTIONISM IS ALWAYS ABOUT THE FUTURE

Perfectionism is always about the future you've decided needs to happen. It's about working hard to make your future better, because the drudgery of living this way now sucks. You may believe the future is supposed to be easy. But for the future to be easy, you would have to stop the behaviors that make life hard right now. Consider the ways you think and act that keep you living up to a perfect ideal. Those are exactly the behaviors that will make life hard in the future, too.

You cannot just drop the traits of perfectionism because you have finally arrived at a long-awaited goal—you have to be aware of them. When you become aware, you need to dig deep to understand what they do for you and then go about challenging the patterns of perfectionism.

This also goes for the situations you choose now. Without awareness about why you do what you do, you will keep choosing the same situations over and over: same results, different day. You'll feel trapped, working hard, with no awareness of what you are actually doing, as you would feel in any assembly line constructing the same product every day.

You may think the universe is trying to screw you by bringing you the same types of people and situations, but it is your doing. You create it by your limited, same old hamburger-with-mustard choices. You don't think it's the burger that's the issue. And it's not! The issue is that you keep choosing it over and over, as a creature of habit. There you remain with the illusion of your "someday funday" reality, rather than ordering the happier meal now.

PERFECTIONISM IS PAINFUL

Beating yourself up is a favorite subconscious pastime for perfectionists. Many of us keep a mental checklist of the stuff we need to do, how we are going to do it, and what might go wrong. If you stop right now to notice the background noise in your head, you might have an uneasy feeling. That could very well be related to an ongoing mental list of things to do. As you're reading this book, you might feel like you should be somewhere else. Hurry up! There's so much to do! Do the laundry, vacuum the couch, get the toothbrush to those baseboards, change the oil, work on that report! Perfectionism keeps you on your toes.

Beating up yourself and others does not change anything for the better. You may beat yourself up emotionally by making more rules, like following a diet of one piece of lettuce a day—oh, and when you are good, you get a teaspoon of salad dressing. You might beat others up by blaming them for what has transpired. You may show it by closing down emotionally, yelling, avoiding, ignoring, and so on. This does not bring you closer to others, and it never resolves the issue.

Let's say you're driving along and this is a 10-second snapshot of your brain: "I can't believe that idiot cut me off! Oh God, Janey is calling, doesn't she know I am still pissed about her sucking the oxygen out of the room the last time we talked? Where's my exit? Crap, I always do this—I get lost whenever I go somewhere new. I am so dumb!"

Look at how everyone in these statements (including you) is less than perfect! And if you have those reactions, I guarantee, they don't just stay in your head. They leak out and control your actions. You are actually treating other people the way you do because of the reaction you have to these types of thoughts. Sure, someone could've done something to trigger you, but your way of seeing things was already in place. No one inserts your thoughts and feelings inside of you. At some point, you have chosen punishment as a tool to distract from what is really going on at a deeper level.

Blaming others is an undertaking you more than likely do on autopilot. You don't realize you're doing it! Blame is a great distraction. When your partner chews too loud and you want to go crazy at the sound, it may not occur to you that you have chosen to be right where you are. You have chosen to be in this relationship with a loud chewer. You can yell at them for their obnoxious mastication, because you expect perfection (and you suffer from misophonia), but it changes nothing.

You may think your desire is about what works for you, and that he or she needs to get with the program. Actually, your expectations of others come from a place of lack or emptiness inside of you. You might see your partner as an extension of you—you judge them like you judge yourself. In your mind, your partner is supposed to highlight how wonderful you are, to cover up that emptiness. When they fail to keep up the pretense, you let them know your displeasure in some way, because you need to get back to feeling okay. "Okay" in this context means feeling numb again, instead of empty. Your partner doesn't realize they are responsible for how you feel inside—how can they, if you don't?

Being aware of perfectionism and the verbal self-abuse that can come from it will not break the pattern, because there is still the fear that drives it. This fear can feel like a train that won't stop rolling: the physical feeling can be hard to put the brakes on. Just having the knowledge won't stop you from kicking your own ass up the ladder, which keeps you pushing, pulling, forcing, or doing what you think is necessary to get to the top. You may see yourself in competition with yourself, or with the other managers in your office. You are first to the team meetings—not only that, but you are in the office earlier than everyone else. And yet, promotion after promotion goes to people you believe are less qualified than you. It pisses you off! What the hell? You internalize your anger, seeing yourself as a loser. It might have you standing at the refrigerator inhaling its contents, or doing whiskey shots outside the gas station. You cannot handle how you feel about you. All the berating in the world will not change your circumstances. It's a painful strategy that doesn't lead to happy.

Imagine you have a goal of being an artist with a following, but for a few reasons you can't seem to make a living at it. You feel unmotivated to create when people want to commission you to do your art—so you struggle, blaming them for what they want. You find that galleries turn you down. The truth is, you spend less time creating artwork and more time criticizing the pieces you do create as less than perfect. So, you don't have enough pieces for a gallery show. Not having the perfect pieces is what keeps you awake at night, but instead of taking action and just doing them, you stay in your head, thinking. You feel like you're standing still instead of being successful.

With all this distraction and second-guessing, is it any wonder there is nothing happening toward your goal? In fact, distracting yourself with punishment for all that is not perfect vindicates you in some way. The more you sell yourself this tale of woe around your artwork, the less inclined you are to move toward the goal.

The cycle of beating yourself up for failing to produce has been around since you were a kid. It's more profound now, with the consequences being that nothing is happening in your career. You want things to be perfect, but at the same time your fear of not being successful keeps you stuck in this cycle of not doing and then justifying your reaction.

Pay attention to your thoughts. They are not only repetitive, but are also looped in a pattern that keeps you from feeling too deeply. Part of the pattern is to stay at the surface level, so you do not end up digging deep enough to get near the root of what drives your perfectionism.

What if, instead, you chose to find out what is really amiss inside of you? What if you examined your thoughts for clues about what is truly making you unhappy?

You need to dig deep into yourself. What is really going on inside when you make a mistake or fail to meet your expectations? Shame, anger, sadness, isolation, worthlessness? This is a reaction. You may not realize that this cocktail of feelings is part of your pattern, but it is—it is something you have tried avoiding. Avoiding is part of the pattern.

Stop avoiding it—be aware. Next time you mess up, sit down, close your eyes, and focus on the physical sensations in your body. What is going on? Perhaps your stomach is tight. Focus on that feeling. What does the feeling say to you? At first it may feel like it is letting you know you are a loser, but if you sit with that feeling, you may notice that underneath it is shame. If you sit with the feeling longer, an old memory might pop up, showing you why you feel shame.

The key is to not judge as you go deeper, but to be curious. Eventually you will get to the negative belief at the bottom of it—for example, not being worthy. At that point, you can now choose. You can choose to take different action in the moment. Or, if that is too far out of your comfort zone, you can just stay with the feelings until they dissipate. Either way, it is about breaking a pattern and shifting a belief that causes you pain.

ON NOT BEING WRONG

Trying to control, aka manipulate, situations around you so that they align with your picture of what's right is another way to deplete yourself of your own life energy. You might believe that the image you have in your mind is the "right way" and others need to get with the program. You might bribe others to go along with the one-way street, but sooner or later they will want to be on a four-lane highway. They have their own list of what motivates them to do what they do, and sometimes it is not the same as what's on your list. You might get a bit upset and wonder why.

It's not that you're a jerk, it's that you have a limited understanding of what the right way means. You picked up this understanding from childhood, from society, and from your own experiences. You needed to believe there was a right way, because it seemed there was hell to pay when you were wrong.

Ick, ick, ick... to being wrong. Can you stand it? I sure could not, for most of my life. I would not even enter into debates with people where I could possibly be wrong. I would clam up! I stepped lightly into conversations, double-checking the topic just to make sure I was right before opening my mouth. For me it was not just being wrong about the subject matter. I am talking about being wrong about how I felt. My feelings never seemed to go along with whatever the popular vote was!

Do you trust your feelings? Or as a perfectionist, or one with perfectionist tendencies, are you also trying to have perfect feelings? Acceptable feelings, ones that everyone else will like and approve of. That way, no one can leave you or accuse you of feeling the wrong thing.

When you feel like your feelings are meaningless to others, it is like hitting a button that says you lack value. This goes straight back to childhood. You could associate it with a loss of some sort—loss of attention, loss of love, loss of acceptance, and so on. You may have committed to rising above the fray and being in the "don't get me wrong" zone. You did not want to be misunderstood; you wanted to be accepted. Acceptance mattered more than anything, so being wrong made you feel like you should just disappear into the ether.

This is why perfectionists have a smaller world, rather than a bigger one. This doesn't mean you haven't traveled or been successful, but in your world, there has been a limited idea of how to get from point A to point B. Perfectionism demands that you stick to the plan—if you don't, you will feel out of control. The plan, of course, is to always be in the right—to keep going in one direction down the road, to make no left turns when your plan says to steer right.

It leaves little room for life to do what life does, and that is to be unpredictable. With perfectionist traits, you are more in tune to patterns than the average Nancy. You expect to be seen in a specific way by others. You keep working to be accepted, or at least not tossed out of the moving vehicle. But we do not control others. We have no idea how other people really perceive us! None of us lives in someone else's body, and until that day comes, we really do not know what others think and feel about us. The following is an example of how being a perfectionist alienated my client Allan, who strove to work harder than his team by proving his expertise so he could receive validation.

Allan owned an architecture firm with two partners. He always had to be in charge and have the last word. He received a major project from a commercial real estate developer. His partners were expecting to help him with this project, bringing their expertise. But Allan struggled to delegate to them. He wanted to make sure it was done right. He didn't trust them, because he felt they were not as committed to perfection as he was! He kept telling them he would involve them as soon as he could. Allan trusted a few of their employees more and wanted to be in charge of who did what. He needed to look like a winner to his client. It mattered to him to win the validation prize. He needed to be responsible for everything—the one to save the day. And really, he also believed his partners were lazy; he felt he would do a better job than everyone else.

Meanwhile, Allan's partners were wondering whose team Allan was on. As I worked with Allan, he came to realize how his expectations and need for validation had him judging his partners. He feared they would make a mistake that would ruin his opportunity to be a shining star. He could see how he never really gave them a chance when it came to major projects. He realized how empty he felt inside and saw how he was trying to fill himself up through his achievements. Inch by inch, he gave up control and invited them in. Allan started to do what would in the past have been counterintuitive: he stepped back a bit. He allowed others to shine and got very clear on his own motivations. As he gave himself more balance and began being honest with his partners, he felt less needy about the client. He started to believe he was on a team, a successful one.

CELEBRATE MISTAKES

Everyone makes mistakes. There is no instruction booklet on how to avoid them. But mistakes don't really have meaning unless we give them meaning. Your mistake may be big to you, but to someone else it is unnoticeable.

The iron fist you may rule yourself with does nothing to help you feel happy. You can celebrate being wrong—being someone who makes a mistake. You absolutely do not need to shrivel up in a ball and fear the worst when you make a mistake like trying to light the oven with the gas on high and singeing your eyebrows (you might need to call 911—but no reason to kick your own ass). Life happens. So, when it does, connect to your feelings and celebrate that you're human. Stop trying so hard and choose to be uncomfortable with your feelings instead.

If you can stick with feeling the unfamiliar sensation of "not performing," you will start to change things for yourself. It's about staying with the feelings while taking different action. Stay connected to the feelings no matter how hard it feels and break the pattern of what you are doing as you are feeling them. If there's no emotion, then taking action alone will not change anything. Those feelings around being perfect need to be dealt with, acknowledged, and let go, while making new choices.

RIGIDITY ≠ HAPPINESS

Wanting perfection means you are pretty rigid. I guarantee there's stringency and a black-and-white perspective to your decision-making.

Often the rigidity around your expectations comes from a deeper need to receive the validation that being perfect brings you.

Look at some of your rigid goals, especially the ones that give you anxiety. This rigidity might give you an illusion that you're controlling things. But control causes problems, with you and with everyone else. When you are a perfectionist, almost every undertaking becomes a problem.

If you are trying to achieve anything that is not based on the feeling of well-being and joy, then happiness will remain elusive. To be happy means you need to be able to roll with it, not be rigidly stuck in your need for things to go exactly how you want them to. Meet Janet—she is rigid and makes most of her decisions from fear; she cannot figure out why she is alone and single when she is such a great catch!

Janet was dating, with the goal of getting into a relationship. Her conditions for the initial meeting were rigid—it must be at this one vetted coffeehouse and she would only meet on Saturdays for a first date. She had a list of required characteristics: he must have a good job, be attractive, like the same outdoor activities she did, listen to the same music, and own his own house. Nothing on her list included emotional availability. She never considered, "Hey, do we like each other?" Janet was very rigid about her list because she was afraid that if the guy did not possess these traits, there would be no hope of a relationship working out.

But when she started working with me, we discovered that the issues went much deeper. Janet feared choosing the wrong guy because she might not look okay to the rest of the world. She also felt a deep sense of lack in herself, which made her create these uptight rules—not just about dating, but about everything. Janet was afraid she would have no control and end up with someone like her father, who for much of her childhood was out of work. The family moved a lot, never owning anything. Her dad never engaged in activities with her that she enjoyed.

For Janet, letting go of her perfectionism meant waking up to the fact that her rigidity was a means of protection. She became aware of her deep sense that she was not worth anything unless she had a man with all the attributes she was sure she lacked. She had never been emotionally open or capable of intimacy, so this was not even on her radar.

In our work together, she became aware of how she created obstacles to her own happiness in love and life. She started opening herself up and being less rigid—allowing first dates to happen in other places and at other times. She let go of her list, broke down her rules, and instead started looking for where she felt connected. Her goal was to be able to be vulnerable and to have emotional intimacy with a man. She met Bob and found him easy to be with. They really connected and are still together.

NUMBNESS ≠ HAPPINESS

Maybe you think that being happy is just for certain moments in time, but true happiness is actually a state of being. You may have confused numbness with happiness because it is characterized by the absence of negative feelings. "Whew! I don't feel bad. What a relief!"

I hate to open up this can of corn niblets, but neither relief nor numbness equate to happiness. And neither relief nor numbness is sustainable (well, unless you are a psychopath). The truth is, feeling nothing is the opposite of happiness. It is unhappiness! Numbness is also misleading. You may be convinced you feel nothing, until you scratch the surface. All it takes is someone to trigger an emotional reaction in you: "Hey, you have broccoli between your teeth!" And *boom,* you may feel shame that you are less than perfect in that moment, and then what? All the numbness went out of the window. Feeling nothing just keeps you in a state of suspended unhappiness.

OVERDOING ≠ LOVE

Do you overdo not only so no one will find fault with you, but also so you can avoid rejection? If you're overdoing for a third-date picnic with someone you really like, you pack eight different kinds of cheese, three types of meats, apples, pears, almonds, sparkling water, still water, two different bottles of wine, a ten-layer cake, and so on. A little much? How is there anything left for your date to contribute? You do this to ensure you are not rejected, but your date may be bored and feel like there is no connection.

To a perfectionist, rejection is right up there with criticism on the list of things that scare the pants off you. You believe you lack the emotional wherewithal to handle it. It can feel like abandonment. In fact, you may react in a pretty extreme way. You might feel as though you are going to die without this person. You can tell yourself it makes no sense to feel this hooked after only three dates, but it doesn't change the feeling. You feel the intensity of possible rejection and you kick your expectations of yourself into overdrive. You also look at your date with certain expectations. You expect them to like you and not leave you—to promise something about the future, to show you are okay. The present moment? What is that?

Back when I had no idea about insecure attachment and my perfectionist ways, I had someone in my life. He had committed pretty quickly, saying this was the relationship he had been waiting for. I ignored every red flag and went into my usual perfectionist ways. I found myself anxious most of the time, because even though he said he wanted to commit, his actions didn't match his words. At the time, I thought I was just not perfect enough—that I was lacking something. This did not mean I chased him or asked him to fill my needs. Rather, it meant that when he tried to tell me he wasn't sure if he could come over one night, I made myself ultra-available—I kept thinking that if he could see how perfect I was, it would all be great! For some reason, it felt like life or death. I went from "I am okay on my own" to acting like a lunatic.

He promised he would call later and let me know for sure if he could come see me. He did not call. I was anxious all night. The next morning, he sent a text. I was so afraid of losing him (losing someone I did not have), I allowed him to say he was coming over the next night. Well, actually I said, *let me get the champagne out* and *I want to make you a surprise*. I baked him cookies. I baked cookies for a guy who hadn't called me, who truly seemed resistant to coming to see me, but I figured if I just was more wonderful, how could he resist?

You can be so far down the rabbit hole you do not know where you are, running for safety by doing what you can to avoid rejection. These feelings are not extreme when looked at from the perspective of a small child who doesn't feel loved, or feels unacceptable in some way. As you have gotten older, you have had those feelings underneath every endeavor, where you hold yourself to some crazy-ass expectation. Each rejection has added to the load of emotional crap you are trucking around in your minivan of pain.

The pain doesn't go away just because you ignore it. Instead, it keeps you looking for that moment of glory when you will finally win the jackpot for all of your hard work. Most of the time, that pinnacle you look toward doesn't exist. It is a feeling you're after. You want to finally be okay, in a place where no one will reject you. Where you can finally ease off your high standards and sit with a drink on the beach. But life never gets there. You keep running the gauntlet of high expectations because you do not know what else to do. Your core fear—whether it's being unlovable, a failure, or abandoned—keeps you overdoing to reach that pinnacle. It's a cycle you stay in until you stop.

What happens when you stop striving and overdoing, and start looking at your fear-based core beliefs? You stop the expectations and find you're happy because you breathe. This takes an unraveling of all that keeps you working so hard. It takes being open to rejection and knowing you are resilient enough to handle it. It takes unwinding the foundation that built your perfectionism.

THE FLAT TIRE OF PERFECTIONISM: IT'S HARD TO CHANGE

At this point, I am guessing you really want to change your perfectionist ways. Being a perfectionist controls your social life, romantic life, and work life. It makes all your relationships more challenging, especially the one with yourself.

NOW STOP TRYING TO BE PERFECT

Yes, you. You are a lovable control freak. Do you hear yourself say, "I'm going with the flow, I'm allowing it, and I'm curious to see what happens." Ask yourself, are you really allowing? Perhaps you find yourself saying to someone, "If you would only do 'this' or 'that'... then everything would be fine!" That's not controlling at all, is it?

True emotional freedom comes from getting rid of the urge to control. Notice the feelings you have about being a control freak. You might be feeling heavy or anxious or resistant.

To stop being a perfectionistic control freak can be difficult. The lizard brain likes you to be vigilant and in control. You might think that striving for control is making your world safe.

But the world is transient. To believe that safety exists outside of you is an illusion. One that you cannot control.

When you focus on rejection, what does it feel like in your body? When you focus on how you work harder than everyone else to control things and yet achieve so little gratification, what does it feel like? Keep asking those questions and look for the feelings of pain or tightness. You might be clenching your teeth or holding your breath. As you feel those feelings, pay attention to what images or memories of past events arise. What do they say about you? Remember that a long time ago, when you were afraid of being abandoned and gave meaning to everything around you, you created a negative belief, based in fear. Going back in time now, you can choose to look at this past event through a different lens. You can choose a whole other perspective, perhaps one based in a more balanced view of yourself. You can see yourself as who you used to know yourself to be, before you created another you based on other people's opinions.

It takes time. Please remember that this work is chipping pieces off the iceberg one chip at a time, not all at once. I often have to remind my clients that they did not get this way in a day and that emotional work takes longer than changing the externals, but the results I and others have experienced have been permanent.

EXERCISE: Stop the Overperforming and Controlling

Grab your journal and set aside about 30 minutes of time. Find a quiet space where you won't be interrupted. You might not see yourself as a control freak or a perfectionist, but try this exercise anyway—you might be surprised at what you discover. It is important to use the tools you learned in Chapter 3 on feeling your real feelings as you answer the questions.

1. Focus on a situation you feel you work hard at, whether it is personally or professionally. Where do you put out a lot of effort to keep things under control or be perceived as valuable? (Examples: You want your partner to treat you how you want to be treated; you want your employees to respect you and do their jobs without mistakes; you want to make the perfect dessert and receive appreciation.)

2. Now, instead of focusing on what you are trying to control by overperforming, see the situation as it currently is. What is the current reality? (Example: You try to be the perfect girlfriend, from giving a great blow job to fixing five-course meals for your boyfriend. He still won't call you or see you as often as you want—no matter how much you try to control in this way. This is the current reality.)

3. Do the body scan from Chapter 3. Do you feel a sensation of physical resistance, pain, or tightness as you see the reality as it is, despite your best performance efforts? (Example: I feel sick to my stomach. I want to throw up. This is how being anxious, sad, or mad feels to me.)

4. Can you see how you try to control the situation by performing? How does it feel? (Example: I feel exhausted and sad for myself that I have to work so hard for so little. I feel disconnected from myself with all that I keep trying to do—I feel like I am going nowhere. I feel totally unlovable.)

5. What scares you about stopping your illusion of control? (Example: He will leave me. I need to keep performing, so he will stay. Imagining what would happen if I stopped makes me feel panicky.)

6. Do you see that no matter what efforts you lavish on this situation, it never changes? Why would another person's reaction to what you do matter? (Example: I see that no matter what hope I have for my girlfriend, she has always overreacted when I do not do things perfectly. Her overreaction makes me want to hyperventilate. I am convinced she will leave me if I am less than perfect.)

7. See yourself committing to continuing what you are doing for the rest of your life, with no change in the situation. What does that feel like? (Example: I cannot handle that, either. Having to work so hard for love and respect, I'd rather live in a cave! I will feel like garbage if this keeps up forever.)

8. Now that you have become aware of your fear and your imagined loss when stopping overperforming aimed at maintaining control, can you stop doing one thing? Pick one activity you can drop. (Example: I will not text asking when I can see him, trying to control communication.) Can you sit with the discomfort of not doing this action? What does it feel like? (Example: It scares me, but it also feels good in a weird way. I feel lighter. I am not trying to control him; I feel like I am taking care of myself. I have more time and energy.)

9. Now look at the whole situation. Having committed to stopping your attempts to control one thing, what "performance" can you give up? (Example: I am stopping the "chef at home" performance of making an amazing meal every night. I am ordering takeout for us both. It feels like he will be mad, but I almost don't care. I feel I am doing something for me. It doesn't matter anyway. I am feeling scared, tired, and unimportant. I feel he notices nothing I do. It will be easier for me to stop performing to get love.)

10. Take one action now, today—whether it is to stop trying to control, or stop performing in some way. Do it and feel it. Start small. Observe how you feel as you go through with it, using your body's felt sense. Remember, lead with feeling and the rest will follow. The more you take these steps, the more empowered you will feel.

As you go through your daily routine, pay close attention to your actions. When you notice yourself overdoing, catch yourself. Ask yourself why you're doing it. Are you trying to control how someone feels about you? Are you afraid of rejection? Increasing your awareness around what you do and why you do it will help break the pattern. BE AWARE.

CHAPTER 6

Step 3—Stop People Pleasing

People pleasing is the drive to control the perception other people have of us so we can show our worth to them, because we don't feel worthy inside. This strategy is manipulative because we aim to gain something from someone else. We want to be seen in a specific way; for example, as a good person. We think, "What would a good person do?" And then we do those tasks for others. People pleasers overgive and please because they fear rejection and abandonment.

The solution is to bring full awareness to the "I am not enough" belief and patterns of behavior motivating this strategy, and learn to feel old feelings of rejection and abandonment.

I PLEASE OTHERS TO BE LOVED

People pleasing is about trying to influence the perception other people have of you through what you do for them. How other people see you matters more than how you feel about yourself. You might disagree with that statement and say, "I don't care what others think of me!"

But the truth is, if someone you care about says you have been abrupt or you've disappointed them, or if they just stopped talking to you for no apparent reason, you have a reaction. Why? It could be that you're afraid of losing them.

Have you ever eaten a meal to please someone? Sounds crazy, right? But research suggests that people pleasing shows up in social situations in some surprising ways. Perhaps you assumed another person wanted you to eat what they were having, to make them happy. If your choice did not come from being hungry or wanting that item in the first place, you were people pleasing.

Pleasing others to keep them in your life is hard, thankless work. You see yourself through what you think is their perspective. You need their attention and validation, and this need can drive you to give away everything (yes, everything!) to them. Deep down, your core belief is that you have no value unless others give you value. You don't feel deserving if you aren't doing something pleasing to earn attention.

The sad part is that you could be pleasing them to win their affection—and perhaps they are smiling and telling you how marvelous you are, while inside, they may be thinking how fake or jerky you are. They might be wishing you'd just sit down and relax and talk to them like a normal human being. You can't know what others think or feel about you, especially if you are doing things you don't really want to do or don't have time for, just to make them happy.

A pattern of people pleasing starts young. All small children want positive, unconditional love. Some of us discovered that the best way to get the love we craved was to please others. In fact, some of us internalized the belief that pleasing others was the *only* way to get the love we wanted.

Remember attachment theory from Chapter 1? As a baby, you are a blank slate. You have no clue about anything except your basic needs being fulfilled: love, shelter, food, and comfort. One or both parents might have been inconsistent, dysfunctional, strict, absent, or overprotective. This inconsistency might have meant you did not know when you would feel loved, and you would form ideas about what you had to do to get love.

Watching your parents and others as models for behavior, you picked up information. You figured out which things seemed to happen repetitively. Perhaps you were called names or told you never did anything right. Nobody put this information inside your body—you gathered clues from the environment and behaviors around you. You decided something negative about yourself, something like *I am worthless*.

So, what to do? You might have thought, "I know, let me clean up Mom and Dad's bedroom. Let me make my bed or do something so I can show I am not worthless." You might have carried this over to friendships, too: "If I am pleasing to them, they will like me!" You gauged whether or not you deserved to breathe based on how much you gave others and what they gave in return. Maybe your dad would give you a pat on the head when you brought him the newspaper. Or pay you for mowing the lawn. Maybe your first love was needy and insecure, and you learned that the way to be loved was to give, give, and give some more.

Your parents, whether they knew it or not, were models of what (in your world) was acceptable behavior. By their actions they demonstrated *this is how you act*. Maybe your mom kissed your teacher's ass to get you a better grade or gave the neighbors a cake so they'd like her, or worked full time and did all the household chores as well, to keep things calm at home. She may have felt angry and depleted but seen no other way to get along in the world. Your dad might have repeatedly helped the neighbors whose cat got stuck in their tree. He may have smiled as he pulled out his ladder, seeming happy to oblige, only to return home and start banging things around in the garage angrily, saying they were taking advantage of him. He kept doing it because in his mind there was no way he could not be the nice guy.

Not only did you witness your parents doing this, you saw it everywhere you looked, with teachers, friends, and other relatives. You wanted to be loved and accepted. Fitting in with others seemed the quickest route there. You understood that you needed to be seen in a very specific way. You learned, "If I am a good person, then others will like me and find me indispensable." You thought, "What would a good person do?" And then you started doing it. Gradually, it became a pattern.

What you didn't realize is that this strategy is manipulative, because your end goal is gaining something from someone else. In this case, approval. But as you know by now, people tend to shut down when they feel controlled.

The irony is that people pleasing doesn't let love in. It might keep people in your life, but it also insulates you from letting others connect deeply. You are constantly seeking validation, doing without being asked, because you believe they will love you more if you run their errands, fill their tank, rescue them from their own crap, and run yourself ragged

Overcoming Insecure Attachment

doing what they want. The fear of abandonment when you have no feeling of inherent value makes you do the dishes for someone else, so you won't end up alone. "But I have to! I can't let anyone down!"

You might even think that keeping others happy will somehow make you happy. It doesn't work, does it? You stay on the screw-yourself train. Every time you please someone as an act of "giving to get," you drain yourself of mental, physical, and emotional energy. It makes you feel more alone than if you did nothing. You are choosing to put other people's needs first, draining your own tank in the hope that you can fill it back up with their validation. But this unconscious strategy is like eating a cheap candy bar. It's a temporary high, and an ineffective and unsustainable form of energy.

People pleasing can affect us in all environments, at home and at work. Richard, for example, worked his ass off in his job as a manager in a large company. He found himself fighting for his staff's wages. Some were deeply appreciative, while two on his staff said "thank you" but continued to treat him and others disrespectfully. He kept them in his department because they were capable workers, but their attitudes were hard to deal with. In a sense, Richard hoped that by getting everyone more money, these two would be grateful, and he hoped that this gratitude would change their behavior.

In addition to fighting for wages, Richard would do other things, like buy his staff lunch once a week and bring bagels in on Wednesdays. He was always trying to do more to create a pleasant work environment, while secretly hoping for harmony. He wanted to be liked.

When we worked together, Richard got in touch with his sense of lack and realized that he thought he was making an impact on others by doing nice things for them. He began to see that all his goal-focused kindnesses made no difference, and that if he was going to do anything, it would have to come from a place of generosity, not to win anyone over. Richard had to look at his feelings about himself and his motivation to try and cover up his own feelings of inadequacy. As he became truer to himself, the situation started to change. The deeper the work, the more outwardly confident he became, less concerned about whether someone liked him or not. Eventually, he let both the workers go, not for personal reasons but because he had the clarity to see that their attitudes affected the quality of their work and the overall health of his division.

EXERCISE: Are You People Pleasing?

Grab your journal and take about 30 minutes of time in a quiet space. Let's do an exercise here. Maybe you're sure that you're *not* a people pleaser. You're just super-generous and give it all away to whoever needs it. Well then, humor me and check out these six questions. Please pay attention to feeling your feelings as you respond.

1. Think of a situation where someone asked you to do something and you immediately had a reaction that felt like a *big no* inside, but you felt a pull toward compliance. Do you feel like you just got punched? Did your jaw tighten or your stomach clench? Do you feel anger? Please describe it.

2. Write down why it is okay for you to feel this pain. Who or what in your past said (by words or actions) that it matters more to do the "right thing" or to keep up appearances than to listen to your feelings?

3. What do you think you will get from the other person by doing this for them? Have you ever felt like you received enough in return? If so, what did that feel like?

4. If you were to prioritize your well-being, how would you have *honestly* responded to the person asking you for the favor?

5. In being honest and not trying to get something (validation) from someone else to feel okay, what do you think you will be giving up?

6. What feelings have you avoided by people pleasing? Can you embrace them?

How did it go? Are you a people pleaser, even just a little? If you are, then read on.

HOLDING ON FOR DEAR LIFE: A FAN CLUB OF NONE

"What do you want to eat?"

"Oh, whatever works for you, I'm easy."

Sound familiar? Having no preferences, as in the above scenario, says nothing about you. People can't get to know you if you don't know or express what you like. Are you afraid to say, "I like steak and chicken" when you're with a vegetarian? Do you think they will be angry, or dislike you? How can anyone really love you or know you, if you don't let your real self be seen?

Being a people pleaser is akin to competing in the Ironman race, but with no medals or cheering crowds at the finish line. There is only you, alone and disconnected. You might not even stop to pat yourself on the back and say, "What an achievement! That was well done." Even if you think fleetingly that you did well, that thought will soon be replaced by another one: "Mary is mad at me because I couldn't help her with her dog Rufus last week when he needed to go to the vet!"

In your mind, you failed. You need that fan club! You're lost unless you are pleasing someone. They might not need you to please them, but you do it anyway. It may be covert, but you want it all on your terms.

My client John lives with Marvin and works from home as a graphic designer. Marvin works for a tech company. Every morning, John starts feeling bad as Marvin shuts the door to leave for work. It bugs the crap out of John that he can't control his feelings of emptiness and anxiety! Marvin's car is pulling out of the driveway. More anxiety comes. Oh boy, he hates feeling needy! His thoughts go into hyperdrive, he is triggered, and he starts wondering if Marvin is stopping by the coffee bar where the really hot guy works. John feels like he's losing himself when he goes down this rabbit hole. He starts imagining that Marvin is leaving him. He knows it is irrational. He knows nothing has happened. But he's getting upset. He starts reviewing how hard he has worked to please Marvin with great meals, great sex, massages, and just being an all-around accommodating guy. Unfortunately, everything he's done doesn't seem like enough to him in these moments.

"What haven't I done?" John asks me in our session. He tells me how he tries to reassure himself when he is triggered: "He won't leave me, I am the best thing that ever happened to him." Then he will send a text to remind Marvin that he exists, going on about the wonderful evening they are planning. He wants to make sure he does enough to keep Marvin locked in, attached to him.

John's biggest fear is that all this people pleasing will still result in Marvin becoming tired of him and his doting. John wants things in return, but Marvin doesn't do as much. At least once a week, John gets to the point where he is pretty worked up about it and confronts Marvin. Marvin gets defensive; he feels he does a lot for John.

I speak with John about curtailing the people pleasing with his boyfriend. I suggest he let himself just be with the discomfort of his feelings, so we can work toward the root cause of his insecurities. I also asked him to be honest with Marvin, telling the truth about himself.

John started sharing his vulnerability with Marvin. This was helpful, because Marvin said he did not want or expect all this effort from John. He wanted to be able to get closer to John but had found it impossible, because it always seemed like John was mad at him. John also shared the insecurity that arose every time Marvin left for work. He explained to Marvin that he did not need Marvin to do anything. John being triggered was in no way Marvin's fault—but it was important for John to share his feelings.

As John opened up about his insecurity and started reining in his people pleasing with Marvin, things started to improve pretty rapidly between them. And with John not depleting himself anymore, he found he had extra energy and was no longer relying on Marvin to fill him up. John also discovered through our work where the roots of his fears were coming from. He was able to break many patterns and shift a few negative beliefs about himself. Overall, John was much happier, feeling relaxed and at ease.

It can be difficult to stop people pleasing. You may feel damned if you do and damned if you don't. The suspicion that you're unlovable if you don't try hard to please controls you and makes you feel needy. But when you think about it, you might discover that if you felt better about yourself, you wouldn't need to balance an elephant on your head. The more you stop the people pleasing, the less attached you are to another person's every move and motive, and the more energy you have for your own life and for true generosity.

MANIPULATION AND FEELING RESPONSIBLE FOR HOW OTHERS FEEL

Manipulation is what happens when we people please. Most of us may not see it that way, but how else do you explain pleasing others to get them to do something for you? You may say, "All I want is a thank you." Which begs the question: Why does it matter? What feelings does it mask inside to hear "thank you" or get something for whatever you did for them?

The truth is, you get to choose how you feel. Not many of us were taught this truth when we were kids. You may be used to ignoring what is going on inside of you, especially if it doesn't fit someone else's agenda. The following pattern, for example, leads to manipulation: "Mom just yelled at me to stop bugging her. What does Mom feel? I better do what she wants, so she will love me."

The manipulation meant to fill us up doesn't work. Instead, stop trying to have your feelings in agreement with others and get to know what is happening inside yourself on a deeper level. When you do, you will no longer feel the need to manipulate others. Even if you previously feared abandonment or rejection, you'll find that what they do or don't do is irrelevant, as long as you do not abandon yourself.

RECEIVING CAN BE HARD

Learning to receive is one of the hardest challenges for someone who people pleases, because you are no longer in control. This makes it extremely risky to accept the gift of coffee in the morning from your lover. You might feel guilt, and it may kick you into, "Oh shit, now I owe them!" No, you don't. The coffee may be an act of kindness from your lover, because they love you. If you feel you owe them, then it is an opportunity to be curious about why.

You are bothered when people give to you without wanting anything in return. You might immediately start thinking about what you can do to even things out. Depending on how insecure you are, you might feel an overwhelming urge to get your previous dynamic back, with you as Gandhi and the other person as the clueless taker. It can be so uncomfortable that when someone wants to do something nice for you, you might subconsciously want to ruin it.

Let's say your guy wants to make you dinner. He buys all the groceries and starts cookin' it up! You watch him, thinking, "Why did he buy peeled tomatoes?! Doesn't he know how to make pasta primavera?"

Cooking is not the issue. The truth is, he is doing something nice for you and you cannot just accept it. It makes you feel insecure, as though he'll wake out of his stupor and say, "Why am I doing this for you? I don't really like you so much! Fetch me a beer!"

The drama triangle might be a factor in your discomfort. Stopping the pattern and accepting kindness moves you off the victim spot, and that can be uncomfortable. Allowing someone to do something nice moves them off the persecutor spot. Your boyfriend can't be the jerk if you accept the concept that he's making you dinner because he loves you. So, allowing this new dynamic can be scary.

PRETENDING YOU HAVE NO FEELINGS OF YOUR OWN

Often, we do not know how we feel unless it is a reaction to how others treat us or how we believe they feel about us. You may also have the sense that with certain people in your life you are always on the defensive, trying to figure out their next move. You may automatically fall into this position without any conscious awareness. You base your actions on past situations, perhaps to prevent anything bad from happening.

In one of my coaching groups, I recognized how many of the group members felt engulfed by what other people thought of them. They had a hard time separating how they authentically felt from their reaction to how someone else was impacting them. When asked how they felt about themselves, their answers were about situations with other people in their lives: "Cary is ignoring me"; "I feel bad and I do not understand why"; or "Margie is paranoid. She makes me think that my boyfriend is cheating on me and I am afraid. It freaks me out!" Or, "Shane keeps telling me that I am overreacting, but I don't think so. It makes me angry." These thoughts aren't feelings, they're fear-based reactions.

The question also opened the door to control issues. Each of them wanted to control a situation with someone else, instead of stating how they authentically felt. They all made statements such as, "I don't want to give them the wrong impression. I don't want them to think I like them. I want to make sure they understand that I am telling them through my actions that there is no hope." These statements were evidence of attempts at controlling and manipulation. By manipulating others, they did not have to experience feelings.

Overcoming Insecure Attachment

The group found it really hard to get to their real feelings. Their way of thinking was to avoid confrontation, people please, and then feel frustrated because things had not changed. One group member said, "I feel so guilty and bad because I am not being honest, but if I was honest she might leave... and as much as I complain about this person, I just can't risk them knowing the truth, or things might be out of my control."

We worked on giving honest information to people. For example, saying, "You are free to do what you want, but I am probably not going to answer the phone because I am busy, tired, or really don't feel like talking." (Whatever they authentically felt.)

When group members dropped their people-pleasing behaviors, small miracles started to happen in their lives. They realized they wanted to know how they truly felt, without being influenced by what they perceived others might think or feel about them.

WTF ARE BOUNDARIES?

Boundaries are not something you impose on other people. Contrary to popular belief, you do not demand people treat you in a certain way. Boundaries are an outgrowth of how you treat yourself. If you are an asshole to yourself, how do you expect other people to treat you? They pick up on your vibe. They can tell you aren't being kind to yourself (even if it is not consciously), and so they, in turn, might not be kind. They might even treat you with a baffling disrespect.

Picture it: What if you're the only one putting forth any effort in your relationship? And the other person is putting in minimal effort—just enough, but very little. You get pissed and demand that they do more, but they do nothing. You keep doing all the people-pleasing moves you have in your toolbox. And nothing changes. You still feel mad, hurt, and disrespected; your partner is still doing what they do.

Why? Because you chose to be in this relationship, working your ass off. You are showing them that it is okay to treat you with disrespect, because you are disrespecting yourself. This is where your learned patterns work against you. Why would you work harder than the other person? Why would you treat yourself so poorly?

Demanding that your boundaries be respected by others is a losing battle when, through your own actions, you are unkind to yourself and discount your own value.

Sheryl, at the beginning of her relationship with Phil, felt that her boundaries were constantly being tested. Phil never needed any alone time and wanted to spend as much time with her as possible. She felt numb to the whole thing, but she believed he was a great guy. She thought he had all the qualities she wanted, so she kept quiet and saw him any time he asked. The more he encroached on her space, the more she felt backed into a corner. She was losing her mind.

But she did not share this with Phil. He thought she was into him as much as he was into her. Over time, she found herself repeatedly starting arguments with him, finding problems. She did this unconsciously, so he would back off and give her some space.

Because Sheryl didn't respect her own need for some space, Phil didn't either. Whenever she started another fight Phil would become a victim, accusing her of not trying to work things out. Sheryl would feel bad and give in. She did not want him to leave.

This went on for 10 years. She never told him the truth.

Inevitably Phil did leave, because he gave up. Sheryl felt like she never got to speak her truth, and that she had suffered for so long only to have things not work out. She tried to get him to come back through making promises and pleasing him. Phil came back once, only to have Sheryl blame him for something. At that point, he decided he was done for good.

This is when Sheryl started working with me to try and learn boundaries. She really had no idea what worked for her and what did not. She was afraid of getting into another relationship and feeling forced once again to do things she didn't want to do. She wanted to work on loving herself, so her boundaries would be recognizable to someone else. Through this work, she discovered what she really wanted, how much emotional intimacy she could handle, and how to stop giving in to what she thought others wanted instead of taking care of herself.

Hurting yourself is something you may be used to and not think about. You might remember your mom complaining about your dad but doing nothing to change the situation. You might see being unhappy but not speaking up as the norm. What boundaries? Fear keeps us in the cycle of hoping someone will change. It doesn't work that way. We must deal with our feelings, the ones we don't think are important enough for us to act on but expect others to stop stepping on.

Having boundaries comes down to knowing what standards you want to live by and how you want to feel in those standards. It's not about wanting the acceptance others can give you, and it's not about waiting for them to change. If you know what feels important to you in your life, such as spending time with people you love, exercising, and eating well—then ask yourself: *are my actions supporting this?* Do you eat well, or do you only wish you ate well and beat yourself up because you don't? What about wanting a million bucks in the bank? Sounds great, but if you do it through people pleasing, overdoing, overcompensating, and feeling like crap then you will not feel good about your actions. You will have treated yourself badly, and your journey to a million bucks is affected by this lack of care. That is disrespect, and if you disrespect yourself, how do you expect others to respect you?

I'm not asking you to be a drill sergeant with yourself. I am asking you what matters. Anything that matters to you will not be achieved through people pleasing. If you want more of what matters in your life, look at how you treat yourself. Making a decision to respect and love yourself through any endeavor is how you change things. I want a million bucks, but I am only willing to work reasonable hours, take care of my health, have some leisure time, and still focus on the goal—I am treating me well.

The key is to treat yourself how you want to be treated. If you recognize your feelings and treat them like they matter, others will treat you and your feelings like they matter, too. And if they don't, you won't hang out. You will say, "I am removing myself from this conversation because it doesn't feel good to me." Your motives aren't to teach them a lesson, they are to ensure you take care of yourself as your own best friend. It's not up to others to determine your boundaries. It's up to you, through your own words, actions, and feelings. Honor yourself and the rest will follow. You will see changes outside of you, and not because you forced your boundaries on other people. You will see changes because you are changing.

SELFISH IS NOT A BAD WORD

Being accused of selfishness is disturbing to a people-pleasing perfectionist. You may believe selfishness means being an asshole. I've heard this from many clients: "If I put myself first, no one will like me. I will piss everyone off, and they won't want to be around me. I'll be the asshole with no friends. I really need to know what others expect of me to be okay."

Maybe your partner gives you a funny look when you say you're going to relax in a bit. You take that facial expression as a criticism and say, "What do you need? What can I do? Is everything okay? I am knee-deep in laundry, but I can stop and make you a seven-course lunch!" It goes back to childhood, for many. When I was a kid, *selfish* was the last label I wanted—it sent shivers down my spine. Being a people pleaser was so much more acceptable. If people pleasing was the way to make others happy, then I would strategize ways to do it.

But looking after your own needs isn't selfish. Focusing on doing for others as a way to control how you are seen is not only manipulative, it's also another way of avoiding your own pain. The *Collins Dictionary* defines selfishness as "self-interest"—the act or instance of pursuing one's own interest. That is not the same thing as being an asshole. According to this definition, selfishness refers to taking care of yourself, knowing your own needs, and filling them. After all, if you don't know your own needs and can't fill them, what can you expect from others?

Being interested in what interests you means that you give yourself attention and treat yourself like you matter. Doing this makes you feel better and gives you more energy. This "selfish" behavior paradoxically means that you have more to genuinely offer others. You can give freely, which makes you less manipulative and self-absorbed.

It can feel risky to stop pleasing others. This loop of not wanting to be selfish, of wanting to be seen as altruistic, is a hard one to break, as exemplified by Jack.

Jack changes the oil for his significant other, Elizabeth. He feels guilty because he has been working all sorts of hours at his job, and Elizabeth is not too thrilled about it. She feels neglected. She doesn't say this; she just appears distant. Jack is tired and did not really want to service her car, but he feels a sense of obligation. Elizabeth outearns him and so he keeps a scorecard in his head—did I do enough? He believes Elizabeth has a scorecard in her head, too. She pays the majority of the bills, while Jack, who is also in school and works full time, is working his ass off to accomplish his goals. Jack loves Elizabeth and really loves being with her. But he keeps hearing his dad's voice in his head, telling him he won't amount to much. He fears that secretly, Elizabeth might agree with his dad. He also fears she thinks he's selfish for spending so much time on work and studies. If he doesn't please her, she might figure he's worthless, and leave him. So he keeps his mental scorecard and keeps doing things for her without asking for help, steadily growing more resentful with every task. He swings between irritation and guilt. All he really wants to do is chill out. But he hopes that if he does enough, his negative feelings will go away.

Jack started working with me after Elizabeth found my podcast. He is starting to share what he is feeling about himself, rather than covering it up. Elizabeth is relieved to see him opening up, because she loves him and could feel the growing distance. She is also opening up, and they are working through their issues together.

Even if you love someone, overdoing is not the way to show it. Putting yourself first is true love, when it is done with compassion. I am not talking about self-absorption or self-centeredness, where you need attention from others at all costs. Putting yourself first means taking care of your interests and ensuring that you are not depleting yourself of physical, emotional, or mental energy. You are conserving it, not needing that self-induced emptiness filled.

With more energy, you can give with freedom. You will realize, "Holy shit, I have the energy of a five-year-old!" It's true—well-being is about feeling alive. If you were on the receiving end, would you want someone to give to you out of obligation, or would you prefer it to be because they genuinely wanted to give? Prioritizing yourself also makes you happier because you're less resentful toward those you people please.

Here are some tips for prioritizing yourself.

- Notice how you feel. If you feel tired, respect that you feel tired. If someone asks you to do something, be honest, say how you feel, and match your actions to your words. Don't say, "I'm tired, but okay, I'll drive you to the stadium." Say, "I'm tired, go ahead and get an Uber or Lyft it or take transit, and have a great night."

- Allow yourself to feel how you do. Don't try to change how you feel to make someone else happy. By allowing yourself to feel how you do without forcing it to change, you find your feelings will naturally change of their own accord.

- What you want has to matter to you; if it doesn't, you aren't your own priority. Act on what matters.

- Commit to listening to what you want and actively do things daily that show you are committed to yourself. This will bring your energy up, too.

- As often as possible, do not do things for others that cause you to resent them. It doesn't bring you closer. It is much easier to say to someone, "If I do this for you, I will not feel good, I'd rather feel good and not make myself angry by doing this right now." And if you end up doing it anyway, be honest with yourself and the other person. Do not lie to yourself about your motivation for doing it, and do not lie to the other person, either. Honesty goes a long way to prioritizing yourself.

If you're a people pleaser, you probably spend a lot of time on the victim and rescuer/martyr points. The people in your life might not see themselves as predators—they might even be your mom, or your kids! But your stepping off the drama triangle will shift their position, and there might be some confusion and resentment coming back at you. Or maybe they'll be glad you're taking some time to prioritize your own needs. You won't know until you try.

The key is to be aware of your own emotions, take small steps, and be honest with yourself and others. The only way to change the situation is to change how you approach it, and this can take time for everyone to adjust to. Be gentle, but don't revert to people pleasing just because everyone's used to you that way. Every time you prioritize yourself by listening to your body, your feelings, and your inner wisdom and making choices that empower you, you take another step toward happiness. The people in your life will soon catch up.

SELF-CARE MOMENT

Give yourself daily moments of fun! Look for the mundane moments, when you are not focused on fun—perhaps turn doing housework into a game, focus on fun moments you can spend together while communicating with your roommates, or learn more about what makes coworkers tick while sharing more of yourself too. The more fun you give yourself, the less compelled you may feel to please in order to get validation from others.

WHAT IS GENEROSITY?

People pleasing is quite different from true generosity. True generosity is giving without strings attached. You aren't concerned whether someone will appreciate you or not; it is the act of giving that gets you off.

You can afford to be generous only when you regularly fill up that space inside of you with your own energy, love, attention, and validation. That is how it works. The feeling of generosity in your body is like a welling up of feel-good emotions. You feel a sense of connection to yourself and to the generous act. We all have moments when we do something from the heart with no expectation of anything in return. That is the fulfillment, the act itself.

Generosity comes from connecting to yourself, whereas people pleasing comes from disconnection: you are strategizing to get a specific outcome. Remember, anything that keeps you attached to an outcome is manipulative. If you give with the focus on getting someone to do what you want in return, it's not generosity. The next time you do something because you have trained others to expect that you will run to their aid when they have a bad hair day, remember that it will not bring you love and fulfillment. It will leave you hungry, like being on an all-lettuce diet. Keep your awareness on what you do and how you feel, notice when you're lonely, and don't deplete yourself further. Take care of yourself by filling up your own tank.

NOW STOP PEOPLE PLEASING

People pleasing is insidious. It takes self-awareness to know you are doing it. Even when you catch yourself, it may be difficult to stop because you've got a lot riding on why you do it in the first place. Identifying your deeper motivation will help you understand your iron grip on people pleasing and allow you to veer away from meeting expectations and onto the white sandy beaches of self-love.

Your deeper motivation to remain in the hell of people pleasing comes from your negative beliefs. Often at the base is an old favorite: "I am not enough." That is a huge driver, along with "I am worthless, stupid, ugly, different, selfish, unlovable . . ." You get the picture.

Unlocking yourself from those handcuffs is essential to your growth. It's impossible to have an authentic relationship with people who have no interest in who you are, how you feel, or what you think is possible. You get to choose how you show up in the world. Examine the real cost of your people pleasing. Have you given up opportunities or wasted time doing for others what they can do for themselves?

Expect some turmoil when you stop people pleasing. You are used to sweeping your feelings under the carpet and acting like they are meaningless. Family and friends may find their feathers ruffled when you start to give meaning to your own needs and stop doing the things they've come to expect. It's okay. They will survive. The relationship will either improve or end. Either way, you'll be happier.

To stop the spiral of people pleasing, you must unearth your deeper beliefs. You do this by feeling your feelings. Think of all you do for others and notice what it feels like. There it is—that heaviness in your chest, or your stomach twisting into a pretzel, or the lockjaw. Going into those physical sensations uncovers a lot. Stay with the feeling. You don't need to change it, just observe it. Use the body scan and triggering exercise in Chapter 3 to help you let those feelings rise, intensify, and dissipate. As an adult, you can handle a lot more than you could as a child. By connecting in this way, you are already starting to break the pattern.

Just knowing whether you are people pleasing is getting you part of the way there. Once you are aware, you can stop lying to yourself and start being honest about your intentions. From there, you will find it easier to start prioritizing yourself as important and doing things that feel good. Even if you think you're being selfish, so what? Really, so what? If you say, "Okay, I am selfish," nothing bad will happen. Lightning bolts will not be flung at you. Saying okay to being selfish will make you take a step back the next time you start to overcompensate. As you keep doing those things you have prioritized for yourself, your own mental, physical, and emotional energy will increase. Your life will start to turn a corner in surprising and unexpected ways.

When you can use your self-awareness to clearly see what it means to dump yourself as a priority and make someone else the priority, you will have stepped out of false hope and self-absorption. You will feel lighter, happier, and freer. You'll find that when you allow some lovin' rather than resisting yourself, you'll feel better, and so will the people who want to be in your life.

If you think people will have a problem with it, then speak up. It takes courage to do so, but tell them, "Look, I have a fear of being selfish, and at the same time I feel you might not like me and so I think about what you want as more important than what I want. I realize it makes me resentful to live this way. Treating myself in this way is misery. I'd rather be able to get closer to you by being real. I'd rather do things for you from generosity, not because I am afraid I will lose you."

Considering your feelings, appreciating your value, and knowing your true motivation will slow you down enough to catch yourself when you fall into that pattern. Just keep feeling your feelings and challenging yourself when your normal response is to run to save everyone. Stop and consider *why* you are doing it. When you do this with feeling, eventually it becomes the new way you operate. People pleasing will be in the past.

Lastly, one other part in getting you to wholesome happiness is to learn to receive from yourself and others. Yes, you are making *you* a priority. But you need to open yourself to the chaos of receiving. Whether it is receiving help, attention, love, a great dinner, or a new pet ferret, learning to receive will definitely be a challenge. It's a challenge you need to work with to be happy.

EXERCISE: Without People Pleasing, How Do You Really Feel?

This is an exercise in awareness. See how challenging it is for you to stop focusing on other people and genuinely know your own feelings. Grab your journal and set aside 15 minutes or longer. Before you start the exercise itself, here are the parameters for answering the question "How am I feeling?"

1. Use only "I" statements.

2. Do not write about feelings being caused through being in a state of reaction to another person or judging what they are doing, such as, "It's because Fred's an idiot that I am feeling this way."

Take your journal and describe where you are and what you're feeling based on you (just you). Get deeper than anxiety and anger or any other general words. Describing and speaking emotions can feel esoteric, but there is value in it.

Example: I feel contented and at ease, which is also uncomfortable at the same time. I feel a sort of giddiness in my stomach—a mix of nerves and excitement. I feel a lightness around my head and shoulders and upper body area. I feel a sense of apprehension that pain will be coming in the future. I feel like I can take a deep breath. This feels like openness in my belly. I feel a niggling sadness and overwhelming grief just over my left shoulder that is a wave I can see coming but don't really want to look at.

The next step is to start getting used to your feelings and talking about them instead of speaking about them as a reaction to others. When your feelings matter, you will see how much less people pleasing you do.

How did that exercise feel? Come back to it frequently—that's how you learn what is going on inside yourself, without referencing what others might be thinking or feeling about you. Remember, how you feel is a choice that you may not realize you made. By doing this exercise often, you will learn how to choose how you feel, which will let you come from a place of action versus living in a state of reaction.

EXERCISE: Filling Up Your Own Tank

For this exercise, take about 10 minutes to focus on yourself in a quiet space. You can always keep your journal handy to take notes.

1. Think about yesterday morning. Can you remember what you did? See if you remember what you spent time doing. (Example: I was at work on deadline; I was running the kids to their soccer games; I was nursing a hangover; I was at the grocery store getting food for the week; etc.)

2. Now look at what, if any, activities you did solely for self-pleasure. (Example: I meditated; I took time to go on a walk; I enjoyed my delicious breakfast; I lay in bed an extra 10 minutes, connecting with myself; I had an honest conversation, which included bonding more deeply; I got a haircut; I spoke with my mom and invited her to a weekend away, etc.)

3. Still looking at yesterday, be honest and ask yourself what activities you did to please someone else. (You can tell what these are because you may have felt angry or exhausted by them; Example: I picked up my friend's dress and drove it 30 miles to her; I worked on a team project by myself; after a meeting I drove a colleague to her house because of her poor planning; I felt guilty for not inviting my boyfriend's mom to dinner, so I ended up inviting her to come stay with us next weekend.)

4. Now, in looking at your activities to please others—can you dig deeply into the feelings that motivated you (guilt, fear, etc.) and see why you would feel that way? (Example: I was worried she'd think I'm selfish; I thought she'd complain about me behind my back; I was worried we'd miss the deadline; I would be left out; I'd be unloved by others.)

5. Ask yourself what you can do to break this pattern in the future. (Example: I can say "I need to take care of myself, and if I were to do this activity, I would feel bad;" I could honor my feelings and speak the truth behind my motivation; I can ask the team to reschedule the project work so that I am not working solo on something that includes others.)

6. In looking at the activities you did for your pleasure versus the ones to please, can you feel the difference in your body? What would happen if you did more activities that feel good inside and come without strings attached? (Example: I would have more energy; I wouldn't be pissed; I'd be scared of what others think, but I believe that after a while I'd feel differently; I wouldn't second-guess my choices; I could be compassionate to others, etc.)

EXERCISE: Being Enough

This next exercise requires some quiet time and a journal. Again, it is important to use the tools you learned in Chapter 3 on feeling your real feelings. You will reflect back to this exercise as you go through the book, to see how this paradigm shifts. Please go through each step, in sequence, and read each step in its entirety before you begin writing.

1. To begin, accept the following basic premise that you are enough:

"I must accept that before I give a thing, or before I receive anything, I am enough just standing here. The act of giving or receiving doesn't change this at all. I am myself, positive and negative, no matter what is happening outside of me. I must focus inside and feel what blocks me emotionally from receiving freely."

How does this feel?

Now, let's examine expectations. What expectations do you have of yourself that say you need to do certain things before you deserve to receive good from others?

Write these in your journal as bullet points. (Pay attention to how they change as time goes on.)

2. Write about how you are becoming more discerning with giving.

For example, "I'm learning to examine my needs, as well as the needs of others, and to see when my gift is truly given from love and when it comes with expectations." What does it feel like when you attach strings to giving? What does it feel like to give with no strings attached? If you are giving with expectations, are they self-imposed or do they come from others? Do they come from needs you cannot fulfill for myself? Why or why not? Write down your responses in your journal.

Having awareness about your motives and the heavy feelings that come with them will help you to be clear before you make an offer of help.

3. Write a list to make room in your life for receiving.

Now take this a step further. Write a list about what you think keeps you from receiving good from other people and from yourself. You may repeat items from the list of feelings and expectations in Step 1. Then ask yourself, "What action can I take to open myself up to receiving?"

Think of all the ways you can receive, whether it is accepting kind words or a stranger's smile or being let into the stream of traffic. Say out loud: "I know that as I receive, I am becoming more comfortable with the art of receiving. I am staying conscious of my feelings and seeing how my receiving empowers those who are giving to me."

4. Write how you feel when you try to relax into receiving.

Write any fears about receiving, such as, "If they buy me dinner, they'll want something. I will owe them!" or "I will not have any power; all my power is in giving."

5. Relax into the feeling of receiving, and write down how this feels.

Now write down how you can relax into receiving. For example, "When my son brought me a flower today, I smiled and said thank you." Feel the difference between this statement and those in question four above, when you might not have been relaxed.

Say the following out loud and notice how true it feels: "I'm becoming okay with the feeling of openness that is necessary to truly receive. It's scary, and I acknowledge it. At the same time, it is less scary each time I allow myself to receive. I allow this open space inside of me to be available."

Please write about your reaction to these statements in your journal.

6. Remind yourself that this is fun and joyful.

As you do this work, remember that these exercises are just reminders—signposts along your journey.

Life is fun and joyful when you stop the mind chatter and expectations you have placed on allowing yourself to enjoy. Imagine giving and receiving—how do you feel? Please write down what it feels like to have fun giving and receiving.

CHAPTER 7

Step 4—Stop Looking for Problems to Solve

The problem-solver has problems to solve 24/7. Problem-solvers do not feel safe unless they're solving a problem or enmeshed in one, often those of others. Their conversations are about problems; their relationships are full of problems. Solving problems makes them feel and sound important. This pattern keeps them from getting close to others, being emotionally intimate with themselves, and making decisions about their own lives.

Breaking this pattern requires you to stop solving problems for five minutes—and this is harder than you think, for a problem-solver. Letting go of a problem without doing anything to fix it takes major work and requires sitting with feelings of fear and discomfort.

ARE PROBLEMS REALLY EVERYWHERE?

Many of us never feel safe in the world—I didn't, and at times I still don't. Seeing material items, including shelter, as a permanent form of safety is an illusion. Holding onto people, a job, or anything outside yourself as a form of security will never bring you permanent relief. In fact, it's what keeps you on the lookout for problems.

When you wake up in the morning, is the first thing you focus on problems? Have you ever heard that what you focus on expands? The more you focus on, say, coconuts, the more coconuts you will see. Soon you're seeing coconuts everywhere. Likewise, the more you focus on problems, the more problems you will see. Whether it's your problem (or your perceived problem), someone else's problem, someone else being a problem, or some circumstance outside of you being a problem, it's all a perception, not necessarily happening in reality. And, in most cases, it's not life or death.

Your reticular activating system is just doing its job. It's a part of your lizard brain, which acts as a gateway from the spinal cord to the main computer. It sorts out information and brings you only the important stuff, like validating your beliefs. Remember, your lizard brain is not concerned with your happiness—just your survival.

In my work, I attract people who are highly intelligent but also best friends with this ancient part of the brain. They're always looking for problems and even creating nonexistent problems, because they don't feel safe unless they're enmeshed in one. It is another way to keep the mind busy, so as to avoid oneself emotionally. They are locked into what I like to call "mental masturbation" and the "What if—?" scenario. "What if blue goo from the sky kills me when I am sleeping? What if some mad scientist is reanimating dinosaur DNA?" Even if their own life issues aren't nagging at them, the ones out of their control will do just as well.

Stop right now and ask yourself what problems you are focused on. Take a moment to write them down. There might seem to be an endless array of them, such as "What if Michael doesn't call me by Friday—then I will have to say adios! But I do not want to, hmmm... maybe I should text him now." Or, "What if Marcia doesn't pay me back what she owes me, then I will have to say something, and it will probably end our friendship!" It might not even be your own issue: "I wonder if Theresa's girlfriend is cheating. I should pay attention. I hope I don't have to be the one to tell her!"

Notice what you focus on. Years ago, I remember reading something in Eckhart Tolle's book *The Power of Now* about not being broke until the moment you go to write a check. When you put ink to paper and realize that you have no money in your account, then you say, "I am broke right now." In the meantime, you might spend a helluva lot of mental and emotional energy stressing out before it actually affects you. Being immersed in problems depletes you of energy. Just like people pleasing and perfectionism, it leaves you feeling awful.

Don't be hard on yourself. You learned this habit as a kid. Imagine being a little tyke roaming around your house and all of a sudden, you're being yelled at for something you didn't know was a problem. Perhaps you took your mom's clean sheets and made a tent? You didn't know you weren't supposed to. Those are always stellar moments in a child's life. Confusion ensues, and Problem-Solving 101 kicks into gear with the lesson "I definitely don't want to get in trouble again—so I better be on the lookout for problems."

This is where insecure attachment can come in. If your parent was hard to deal with emotionally, giving you loving attention and then taking it away seemingly at random, their inconsistency will make you wonder if it is you. It puts you on high alert, looking for possible problems in your environment. You fear losing their positive attention and gaining negative attention, or being ignored. Dad might talk to you in a nice voice on a Saturday morning, then ignore you completely on Monday night when he's in front of the TV. You are wondering what you did. You might think it's the TV—maybe it's more interesting than you. Maybe you're just a bother. Or maybe your dad has his mind on stuff from work and is completely checked out. You might think you can only have your dad's attention on Saturday mornings, but then next Saturday rolls around and he doesn't blink an eye in your direction. You may go through life looking for situations that mimic this dynamic, as an unending problem you try to solve. In reality, your actions probably had little to do with his intermittent attention. Let's meet Lainey, who focused on problems with her partner to the point that she almost talked herself out of remaining in the relationship.

Lainey had been dating her girlfriend for about a year, and she was struggling. She would say, "Michelle is great! She's calm, sweet, reassuring, and positive! She's always available for a call when I need her." But Lainey felt totally stuck, because as great as Michelle was, all Lainey could focus on were problems—specifically, Michelle as a problem. She caught herself fixating on ways she didn't measure up. One of the ongoing problems was that they didn't spend enough time together—only about three days a week, including weekends. Plus, Michelle was always late, she wore the same pair of pants every time she saw her, she bit her fingernails, and her cat was irritating.

Lainey believed these were all serious issues. As we worked together and she started to feel her feelings daily, she felt better. But she still had her "problem detector" and it still went off the rails every time she saw Michelle, or when she knew they weren't going to be seeing each other. She found herself angry with Michelle for a particular quality, or for what she was or wasn't doing. She was in tears of frustration at feeling that she could not accept Michelle as she was. She understood intellectually that Michelle wasn't doing anything wrong, but emotionally she always seemed to be building a case against Michelle, so she could leave her. Deep down inside, when Lainey was in touch with her feelings, she felt that staying with Michelle was the right choice. But she did not trust herself, and she worried that her inability to trust her choices must mean something was wrong with the relationship.

In Lainey's case, looking for problems with Michelle came down to the fact that she did not accept herself. She felt that Michelle was better than she was, while Michelle seemed so sure of both the relationship and Lainey. As we worked together, she began to see all her insecurities about being good enough. She'd been trying to avoid that insight by focusing on Michelle as the problem child.

As Lainey started to value herself more by speaking up truthfully (not complaining or accusing Michelle of anything), by looking at why she was unhappy with the amount of time Michelle gave her, and by seeing her other expectations clearly, she started to get a clearer picture of herself and her need to control. She pulled back. Instead of focusing on Michelle, she dug deeper into the source of her perception. As she started to take responsibility and treat herself better, the relationship changed. She felt happier and freer, and so did Michelle. In fact, she soon started spending more time with Lainey. Now they are engaged to be married. Lainey still has to be aware that when she's looking for problems where they don't exist, it more than likely means she is avoiding her feelings or out of sorts with herself. Now she knows to go there first.

Problems are multifunctional. What about your career? You might spend an astronomical amount of time enveloped in problems when that is your job. You are a paid problem-solver! You are a metal detector, checking your environment and the people in it for anything that could lead to a problem. What about your relationships? Maybe you notice the look of dissatisfaction on your mom's face at your favorite restaurant and think, "Oh shit! Here comes the problem. She is not happy, and she is about to make a scene with the waiter! Yikes! I'm not going to be able to come back here". You might try to talk her off the ledge and stop the fireworks from happening. You do this on autopilot with everyone—even strangers. Figuring out where their problems are just by their body language, you are hopeful you can either solve their issues or bond with them about it. Yeah, some kind of wacky bond with someone you don't know, commiserating over a similar problem. It makes you feel better about yourself, so why not? It's validation.

It's not that problem-solving is a horrible thing, but when it becomes your favorite pastime, then it is a problem. There's also a bigger threat to your happiness: Problem-solving worsens over time. The more you look for problems, the more afraid you grow of life. Your world gets smaller and smaller. It's not living. It's not happiness, and you've been there, done that.

THE PAYOFF OF FIXATING ON PROBLEMS AND SOLUTIONS

Insecurely attached folks, or more specifically, those who are avoidant and anxious in some capacity, are expert problem-solvers. They have great confidence in themselves in this role, because it is safe to be in problem-solving mode. It's safe because if they're the one solving problems, they can't be the problem. Right? "I am the guru on the

mountain, bring me your problems, oh weak and withered people!"
Right.

The mind loves problems. It is like a computer you are feeding a connection to, while disconnecting from your emotions. You might be so
good at problem-solving that everyone calls you looking for advice.
This allows you to fill your focus with other people's problems. But
how do you feel about the people you're helping? You might feel that
you never have to get close to them; after all, they're people who aren't
bright enough to figure out their own solutions. This gives the benefit
of superiority. It works for those who want to avoid getting close to
people. One way to do this is to always be rescuing or fixing them. As
an anxious or insecurely attached person you may also need the validation of solving others' issues. Either way keeps emotional distance
between you and others.

We all have people in our lives who whine and complain. We call them
a downer. They're a downer because they don't want to recognize that
they're creating problems, with no desire to change. Everything in
their lives is a problem: "My dog has fleas"; "I hate my alarm"; "I never
buy anything good to eat"; or "My husband doesn't listen to me." They
bring up problem after problem, an ocean of problems. They live in a
constant state of life as a problem. They're anticipating problems that
haven't even happened yet.

These people are annoying, but they're also familiar. You know what
to expect—no surprises. It's safe. It's comfortable. It requires no real
emotional intimacy and keeps you disconnected, thinking, "I know
what you're going to say, I know what you're going to do. This is going
to happen, and I'm going to say what I always say, and it will have a
certain outcome." You can check out and sip your beer. And you can
avoid your own issues while helping them with theirs.

You might be playing out the drama triangle too, acting as the rescuer. It's a slippery slope from there to becoming the martyr/victim.

Safety comes up in another way here. The delusion is that nothing can bite you in the ass when you're always in problem-solving mode. Even if a situation isn't yet problematic, believing that you are already solving the problem that doesn't yet exist lets you relax, because you're one step ahead. You have won! It really doesn't matter if the situation turns problematic because you now have the solution in your little bag of tricks, just in case. It gives you a sense of false confidence. You put your trust in your mind to figure things out, but your mind has not had the experience. It can't see every possible ramification or outcome of a situation. Sometimes problems actually lead to a better situation, if you're not running around trying to solve them prematurely, controlling the outcomes. Life can't be controlled, and an unexpected nightmare can come out of nowhere. How confident are you then? Do you feel like you're totally screwed?

Only when you are emotionally resilient can you really trust yourself to handle a problem confidently. And that's because you're not trying to handle the problem intellectually or anticipate and preempt potential imaginary problems. You will allow a situation to unfold before you rush in. At that point you will usually find that unless it's a burning building, you don't need to rush anywhere.

DROWNING IN BS

Old, old, old patterns are hooked into why we get stuck in problems.

Remember childhood? What did your parents spend a chunk of their time talking about? Was it all the wonderful things in the world, or was a major portion of it devoted to problems? Did they seem happy?

Perhaps they were temporarily relieved when a major problem was solved, but did you notice they moved onto the next problem? It's a pattern, and you might have picked it up. You might perceive the world as one problem after another, without any conscious awareness that you are doing this.

What if you are Charlie the complainer or Marge the meddler or Frank the fighter, always struggling with problems? This can change, but the first step in changing it is recognizing problem-solving as a heavy, soul-sucking focus.

Of course, a lot of this behavior is on autopilot, hard to see until you become aware of just what you are doing.

I had to be honest with myself. For years, I would listen to people in my personal life talk about their problems. The familiar drone of their issues would keep me occupied. I never would have admitted that I felt superior, but it did give me that edge. You might also feel superior to the person suffering in the moment when you're out of the fray, problem-solving from on high. The bigger issue that became clear to me was that this sense of superiority helped me avoid my own issues. I didn't have to deal with how insecure I felt. *Let me solve your problems for you, aren't I wonderful?* For a long time, I did not see this knack for avoiding myself while simultaneously trying to make myself feel better, but it was the dynamic I set up with others. And yes, I did care about them too. It wasn't coldly intellectual, but there was a comfort level in knowing I could excel here.

What finally changed was that I wanted to be happy. This desire changed everything, because I had to stop looking for problems—mine and everyone else's. Do you want to be happy? Of course you do! Will being Dear Abby help with that? No. Nothing happy is happening when you are constantly knee-deep in problems.

Who are you without your problems? To find out, drop 98 percent of the things you call problems, the issues you may focus on without even being aware you do it. Feeling bad may be your normal. Many of us never had a true sense of well-being. There may not be a memory of consistently feeling good. I never felt good consistently until I started addressing all this stuff. I would wake up and go to sleep focused on problems. My own problems I would try to gloss over or solve expediently. I wanted others' issues, so I could fill my brain with something, anything but how I was feeling.

Now I no longer focus on problems. In fact, I lose interest 99 percent of the time. My lizard brain is on decompress; I rarely encounter it unless I have an issue right here, right now, that I need to resolve, like a flat tire. I'm not running around trying to problem-solve in the future or making problems in the present to keep my brain occupied. I'm totally with reality.

It's okay to switch gears and stop focusing on problems. The world will not fall apart. It is scary—and who knew shifting your focus to meaningful things in your life could be scary? But it is. It's unknown. To shift your behavior means living in the land of "I don't know." "I don't know if that is a problem," "I don't know what will happen in an hour," "I don't know the answer," "I don't know if things will work out as I picture," and so on.

When I say those statements confidently, I am living in the here and now. I've stopped focusing on problems. I let life work it out. And unless it's happening in this exact moment—*is it an actual problem for me right now, right here?*—what I'm basically doing by not trying to problem-solve prematurely is freeing up all this energy. My mental, emotional, and physical energy gets to cut loose instead of being wrapped up in problems 24/7. That, my friends, is movement toward permanent happiness.

EXERCISE: Is It Really a Problem?

Take your journal and find a quiet space to write for 10 to 15 minutes. Remember to use the skills in Chapter 3 to feel your real feelings.

1. Right now, think about one problem you have been focusing on lately. Do a body scan to identify any physical feelings that come up.

2. Now get deeper. Ask yourself, "Why have I been focusing on that particular problem? What am I avoiding in myself?" Take a moment to feel what comes up. Where do you feel it? Maybe it's a hollow feeling in your chest. By feeling your way through it, you should be able to get a picture of what it is you're actually avoiding. You might come up with an answer like, "Well, if I focus on all this drama out there, then I can avoid the fact that I don't respect myself."

Here's an example of how that exercise can help you move beyond surface problem-solving to deeper realizations.

My client Julie was living in temporary conditions. One day, Julie saw a photo of her roommate on Instagram, wearing an outfit identical to one Julie had hanging up in her bedroom closet. What?! Julie marched into her closet, saw the outfit hanging there, and pulled it off the hanger. It looked and smelled like it had been worn. Her roommate had borrowed her clothes without asking and hung the outfit back up in her closet without saying a word.

On the Richter scale of problems, it's not a huge one. But she went ballistic: "How dare my roommate do that? It's so disrespectful! She didn't ask, she doesn't value my things, she's a jerk and an entitled spoiled brat." On one level, Julie's feelings make sense. It would have been simple courtesy for her roommate to have asked before using her clothes.

But simple on the surface often means deeper issues underneath. As I prodded Julie to go deeper emotionally and not avoid the truth, she started crying. She felt awful about her choices. Not only did she have no control over her belongings, she felt she did not have much of a choice about where she was living. She felt powerless. She said, "I don't really have to focus on the fact that I fucking hate living here and I hate my life because I am not where I want to be, right? I mean, my roommate is an asshole for not asking, but that's just the tip of the iceberg."

Avoiding reality and focusing on small problems has a huge payoff. You don't have to tune into your deeper issues; you can just stay distracted by other ones. Every time you avoid going deeper to see what is making you a ticking time bomb, you give yourself permission to remain numb. But the unrest is always beneath the surface, centered in the problems you do not want to face, never mind solve. The disharmony inside does not go away because you ignore it. It is *there* because you ignore it.

I lost my job at the beginning of the economic downturn. I was losing my house, a place for my kids to be (even though they were older), most of my belongings, and a sad-ass relationship all at once. I was finishing training as a coach at the time. I could avoid the real issues like money, shelter, and my internal crap as to why I was in this pickle, placing my whole focus on the dysfunctional relationship I was in, while coaching other people. I could be the advisor while my world fell in the toilet. I could avoid my real issues—the fact that I was anxious 24/7, crawling across the floor at times. To me these things did not seem to need my attention. I was emotionally compartmentalizing my problems. I was in survival mode, and I could absolutely not deal with how screwed up my life was—I focused on an illusion of a relationship while my life went up in flames.

If you suspect you are using surface problems as a way to avoid your real problems, you will want to get familiar with what triggers you. Is it really that you wake up focusing on problems? Is it just your way of life to jump from one to another? What do you deny to yourself when it comes to how you are creating a lack of harmony? The little voice inside your head whispers this to you, but you may have tuned it out. Now is a great time to really tune in!

BEING A PROBLEM DETECTIVE

Some of you could get your PI license and open up shop! You may spend an inordinate amount of time figuring things out: "Give me a problem and I will analyze the hell out of any possible solution! I need distraction from myself and what I am doing, so give me all the clues and I will cobble together a story!"

Believe it or not, there is a benefit to being a *problem detective*. In fact, there are three benefits:

1. It places you in the future, so you're not in the present emotionally–a nifty way to avoid yourself and whatever is currently happening.

2. It helps create the problem. Remember: what you focus on expands. If you focus on the possibility of a future problem, what do you end up doing? You end up creating it. Your actions, words, and distorted sense of reality will have you believing what you're telling yourself. You'll be making a problem happen. In believing "my girlfriend's going to cheat," you're suspicious, so without permission, you go through her phone and question her every move. She might not cheat, but I guarantee that at some point she'll do something you'll see as proof that you shouldn't trust her. This leads to the third benefit of being a detective:

3. It's a self-fulfilling prophecy. Now you can prove, again, that there is a problem, which fits nicely with the evidence for your negative beliefs about yourself: "I'm screwed. The universe hates me. Everybody's an asshole. I am unlovable. This world sucks." You win, you're right! Unfortunately, being right gets you nowhere near being happy.

It can come down to a lack of trust. This problem (which might be imaginary) may give you an excuse to shut down, thereby killing off your relationship without you ever suspecting you were the driving force. It keeps you in the clear from having a real bond with someone. Being a detective is not love-based. Ninety-eight percent of the time, the stuff in our heads never happens the way we think it will, as was the case with Jeremy:

Jeremy thought he might be getting fired. His boss seemed to be avoiding him. He talked to his friends about it, asking what they thought. Remember, he was talking about a problem that hadn't happened yet. One friend suggested kissing his boss's ass, another friend proposed snooping around his office, and yet another friend said Jeremy should get the down-low from his secretary or his other coworkers. A fourth friend said he should start looking for another job.

Jeremy didn't know what the problem was. He couldn't predict how it would turn out, but he created it! After a few days of Jeremy making himself anxious and crazed, trying to find a solution, his boss called him into his office. He told Jeremy that he knew he'd been distant; he'd just been busy with new plans for the unit. He then went on to say that Jeremy would be promoted from his current position.

Was it opposite day?! Wow... his boss communicated with him—no problem! What does that say about all his wasted detective work?

Evidence. Your lizard brain holds many negative beliefs. These beliefs are always looking for evidence that they are justified, and that all is not well. It's pretty handy-dandy to be a detective employed by your belief system. You put your energy into finding the problems, to prove a belief. The belief will jump for joy as you are stuck in your autopilot patterns and start to do what you can to undermine yourself and prove it right! In Jeremy's case, he believed that he wasn't good enough and assumed that his boss was ignoring him because he was about to be fired.

But playing detective is tiring. You don't ask the questions, because you fear the answers. Why do you fear having the wool pulled over your eyes? Is that what you feel you deserve? You'd rather not know for sure so you can avoid disappointment and strategize your way around solving a nonexistent problem, keeping yourself too busy for real reflection and insight.

There is never a reason to do detective work, looking for problems where none may exist. It is easier to let things play out how they will anyway. If you feel there's an issue, then ask the question.

NOW STOP LOOKING FOR PROBLEMS TO SOLVE

By now you can see how looking for problems is like a cul-de-sac: you just keep driving in circles, looking for the same address on the same road. You can also see that the *why* comes from fear. Fear drives us to find problems, thinking we're keeping ourselves safe. It may now be clearer that if left to their own devices, many perceived problems will self-correct, or were not problems to begin with. I let problems go all the time, because most will clear themselves up. And letting them go clears a path for more pleasure.

Now, there are times when a problem needs some attention. It's often because there's a choice to be contended with. But it doesn't require your entire focus, unless it is life or death. Solving problems does not equal happiness; solving problems offers relief. Relief is not joy.

Take the case of Rachel, who was on a dating app. All she could see were problems. None of the women seemed to be a good match. One of the women said she loved diet soda, and Rachel not only decided that she was not a match, but that she needed to tell the woman that what she drank was unhealthy. On the rare occasions when a woman she had not discounted was available and they'd start seeing each other, Rachel would ignore red flags such as, "I am not over my ex," or "I am not sure I can handle a relationship." Then she would find herself in a relationship where there was one problem after the next. You could say Rachel was looking for problems.

Many people have the idea that safety will come from being rescued by some solution they have not yet come across. This desire for rescuing stems from childhood, and it's natural for kids to look to others to rescue them.

Overcoming Insecure Attachment

But the only way to be rescued as an adult is to recognize that our safety is located inside of us—we are with ourselves 24/7. It's not about solving all your problems; it's about getting to trust that you are emotionally okay no matter WTF is going on.

Safety is within, and it comes when you make decisions that are in alignment with your deeper true feelings. The true you is the person buried beneath all the conditioning. Feeling safe inside is possible. When you feel safe within, you do not wake up feeling like there is a problem you must solve. You go through your day without looking for or asking about problems. You do not jump in and problem-solve with others just to keep your focus on something else.

Instead, you find yourself feeling quite calm and peaceful. You notice your stomach isn't tight, your jaw is not clenched, your shoulders are not hunched in problem-solving mode. Your body is relaxed. If you feel something out of whack, then you just sit with the feelings.

EXERCISE: Moving Away from the Dependence on Problems

Even if you do not believe you are a problem-solver, we all have tendencies to distract and get caught up in issues. It is valuable to everyone to have fewer problems encumbering them. Grab your journal and take 30 to 45 minutes of time in a quiet space. For this exercise, it is important to use the tools you learned in Chapter 3 on feeling your real feelings. Use your journal to record your replies to these questions. Please take your time.

1. Let's identify and challenge the ways you submerge yourself into problems. Make bullet points in your journal, listing the bigger problems you focus on—the ones that are repetitive.

2. Do you notice how you feel about having those problems? Use your felt sense and go into your body to identify where that feeling sits. Describe it.

3. Consider how safe and familiar problems might feel. Does it feel normal to be looking for and focusing on problems?

4. Look at your bulleted list of problems. Is there actually something you must deal with right now? Mark with a check mark. Are there some problems that may or may not happen? Mark those with an X. Can you tell which problems are a current reality and which ones aren't?

5. Think about how it might serve you to focus on a problem that hasn't happened yet, or might not happen. Write down any benefits you can see.

6. Review the list of bulleted problems again. Which ones belong to other people? If there are any of these, what does focusing on them allow you to do?

7. Think about what you are afraid might happen if you let go of focusing on problems. Can you see how focusing on problems creates distance between you and yourself? Can you see how it is a wedge between you and others?

8. What sort of outside validation do you receive by hanging onto a problem or playing detective to find a problem?

9. If you were to look at something you have labeled a problem, would a neutral observer see it the same way you do?

10. If you stopped making problems your focus, how would that affect your relationships? Sit and feel the sensations in your body to identify the relationships most affected by focusing on problems (real or imagined) inside the relationship. How would it feel to have those problems shrink or disappear?

Give yourself time. Really look at your need for safety and understand how you can get there by being connected to your own emotions. Of course, loosening your grip on problems will also help you to feel better.

Consistency is something you will build going forward, as you begin to drop your problem-seeking and problem-solving ways. The more you find a more joyful focus, the easier it will become. You will feel lighter and more energetic, and that will help you to stay aware and be consistent in your own behavior. See yourself being consistent, showing up, being 100 percent you, not worrying about the future or the roof caving in. What does it *feel* like? A mix of feelings? I would imagine so.

When you really stop focusing on problems, things are a lot simpler. You feel better without the constant alarm bell going off, signaling another problem. It allows you to connect to yourself—to know how you feel and what you truly want, and to convey your truth to others. This relaxed approach becomes second nature, the more you focus on feeling good. And this is where life becomes magical. Building your value comes from having your energy back in your body.

In an unhealthy relationship, the focus is always on problems with the relationship, with one or both of the people in it, and with the situation. The drama triangle comes into play, and you can cycle around its three corners for years as you shift focus from one problem to the next, year after year.

In a healthy relationship, you actually don't focus on problems most of the time. When you do, it's a real problem like, "Oh, you lost your job," or "Oh, somebody's sick."

In a relationship with yourself, the same thing applies. Having a healthy relationship with yourself means trusting that all is well and dealing with your feelings as they arise. Staying connected to yourself means that if a real problem arises, you know how you feel, and you can take appropriate action. Until then, you can relax. Problems don't have to be a permanent part of your psyche—take them out of the limelight and get to living!

CHAPTER 8

Step 5—Stop Going against Yourself as a Victim/Martyr

Those of us who go against ourselves say yes when we mean no and vice versa. Often these folks choose to be a victim or a martyr (rescuer). Going against ourselves is a slippery slope to personal hell, because we feel a ton of anger and resentment toward others. We've put our needs last and we do not even know what our needs truly are, most of the time.

The solution is to become responsible for your choices—to own your decisions. You learn to give up the rules of "going along to get along" while discovering how to trust yourself and your needs.

HOW HARD IS IT TO SAY WHAT YOU MEAN?

This chapter uncovers why you may choose not to consider your desires.

Let's start with the example of Andrew. Andrew had been a musician since he was a kid. He spent most of his spare time playing the piano and writing music. He played in bands as a teen and had some minor success. In his twenties, he moved with his bandmates to LA. They struggled for a few years trying to become rock stars, then Andrew found himself a job. He decided to concentrate on making a living, but he still hung out with his bandmates and played with them once in a while.

One night at a club, after they finished playing, they were approached by someone who wanted to manage them. Just what they wanted! Their new manager said he had an opportunity for them, a six-month, cross-country club tour. Andrew struggled mightily but felt that choosing his dream would be too scary at this point. He was committed to his job. The dream of being a musician was in his rearview mirror.

Andrew didn't leave town with the band to go on tour. Instead, he focused on working, got married, had kids, and bought a home. He still played piano for fun, and one day he decided he wanted to perform live again. His kids were a little older, so he had a bit of time. Once again, he started performing and once again, he was given an opportunity to perform elsewhere, but this time it was just for one day—a workday. He really had a difficult time; he wanted to say yes so badly, but he felt that taking the day off would be irresponsible. Besides, he was not in a position to pursue a career in music. In the end, he chose against himself.

When I started working with Andrew, it soon became clear that his fear of success went back to childhood. That was where he learned to choose what he thought was the "right thing" to do, even if it felt bad. He'd wanted to be a musician forever, he was talented, he had been given opportunities, yet he'd repeatedly said no and let his dream go. Each time he denied his own wishes, it was a struggle. Finally, he was ready to make a change, start a career as a musician, and confront his old fears.

SELF-CARE MOMENT

What is a dream you still have and have not acted on? Take one baby step a week or a month toward it. Baby steps will make it easier to deal with the fear that has stopped you from doing it.

Denying yourself what you deeply want comes from listening to those sneaky negative beliefs that you're not enough, or not good enough, or don't deserve to be happy. They are really telling you that you must wait for permission to choose yourself.

The drama triangle discussed in Chapter 2 often comes into play when you choose others' desires while putting off your own as unimportant. You may have a long history of being a martyr/rescuer for someone else, choosing against yourself while you help them, looking for validation or some other external reward.

You don't feel better when you strand yourself in the middle of the desert. You might feel the world should have ESP, knowing that you are on your best behavior. *Yes, I brush my teeth twice a day and floss; I eat an apple a day; I helped someone cross the street; I got straight As.* How much do you have to do before you will possibly feel you have earned what you want? Putting your own needs on the back burner places you into a state of sacrifice and suffering. You may have watched Ma and Pa model this behavior, along with your own experiences, learning that you and your feelings didn't matter so much. All of this will absolutely keep you on this merry-go-round. It can be exhausting, feeling that you don't deserve your own rewards.

Only you can decide to commit to your happiness. If you don't make that commitment, who will?

When you make a commitment to yourself, your words, actions, and feelings should match. So if, on the podium in your mind, you adamantly state your strong desire for something specific, then 30 seconds later something happens and you rescind your commitment, you need to delve inside yourself and figure out why.

Some examples of self-sabotage include:

- You say you want to be fit, but you eat a dozen donuts before 8 a.m. and are in a sugar coma the rest of the day. Then you struggle with self-recrimination and shame.
- Most days, your baseline emotions are anger and resentment, since you sacrifice your choices and feelings.
- You feel like you've been waiting your entire life for permission from someone or something to tell you that you've earned the right to do what you want.
- You really believe life is black and white—no gray. It's either right or wrong.
- Even if you really want to do something, a million obstacles stand in the way.

This is a real dilemma. But you have a choice. You can continue to ignore your feelings, mistrust yourself, and believe that you don't deserve the life you want. Or you can switch gears, stop basing your actions on a version of "the right thing to do," stop prioritizing others' hopes or expectations, and move inward to honor your own sense of well-being.

It's pretty easy to choose the second option when you see it put like that, isn't it? I mean, you already know what life looks like when you don't value yourself. And yet, even the idea of building your own value can feel esoteric and challenging, because of how many entrenched patterns you will have to overcome.

It truly is the patterns which keep us feeling bad. Angry. Resentful. Building cases against other people. Waiting for them to wake up and see what's happening. Perhaps even believing that you are totally in touch emotionally, and that it is everyone else who is screwed up. But these patterns have to be looked at, identified, and changed. If you do not have your deeper goals, feelings, thoughts, words, and actions aligned, then you will continually go against yourself. If you are waiting for permission from someone else, or a verdict that you are okay, that you should be able to do what you want, then you will be waiting a long-ass time. Even if someone gave you permission, it doesn't mean you would actually take action. It is still an internal choice. So, you will keep making sacrifices that feel bad, and you won't be inhabiting the life you really want—it's like wearing a tuxedo for a day of tanning at the beach.

Again, the good old lizard brain and attachment theory have a role to play. You might not even be able to see that you have choices. You might feel that there is only one way to do so many things in your life, because of what you learned as a child about the world and your place in it. Every time you come up against the unknown, you shrink back into the world you are familiar with. The "known" feels heavy, depressing, and repetitive, but at least you know what to expect. You come to believe even more that life is not in your favor. Then you believe that you have fewer choices than you actually do. In a few years, you believe you have fewer still. You might as well be in prison. In fact, you already are.

The good news is that the prison was built through conditioning, and you can change it.

YOU'RE YOUR OWN WORST ENEMY

You may believe that you want a relationship, a job, your own biz, or something amazing, but without knowing what lurks in your belief system, self-sabotage is covert. You don't see it! When you don't get what you want you might get frustrated, shaking your fist, believing things just happen to you. Little old innocent you, mmm hmmm. The truth is, you're standing in your own way. The unknown is powerfully scary, so as frustrated as you can get about standing still, you adapt and deal with it. It's what humans do—we are adaptable creatures, until we get triggered out of our tree.

To change things, you have to become your own best friend. Your own value has to matter to you. It has to matter enough that you're willing to get really uncomfortable and change what you do. If what you say and do doesn't match what you really feel, then your self-awareness is probably a little malnourished. You're used to focusing your awareness elsewhere. If you switch your focus to yourself, you may find that what you believe you want is not what comes out of your mouth, and isn't reflected in your actions. Self-sabotage happens, and it leads to self-fulfilling prophecies. "I really want a relationship! Okay, so I am gonna go on a date tomorrow? Oh, wait. I'm getting a cavity filled. Maybe next week." *We do this all the time.*

Pay attention to what you say you want. Before you know it, fear is like a ventriloquist—it's taken over your mouth: "I want to lose 30 pounds. Oh, you're ordering pizza, please get mine with the works!" You don't see what you just did, but you feel it. You start making excuses and rationalizations in your mind, things like *just this once*. The pizza arrives and you inhale it before you realize what you're doing. Once you wipe the last crumb from your mouth, you are flooded with shame and guilt. Self-loathing takes over, and you go to battle with yourself.

Self-sabotage is a pattern. Your lizard brain believes it's protecting you from change. It's rarely consciously deliberate for you to break your commitment to yourself. Half the time you can't understand your motivation. Would it kill you to miss the pizza? No. So why did you pig out? You don't really know, and that can drive you crazy and have you beating yourself up for the rest of the evening.

YOUR SHRINKING WORLD

After a while, small world isn't just a ride—it becomes the reality you live in. The smaller the world, the more overprotective your mind gets, trying to stop you from engaging with anything unknown, which could possibly be uncontrollable or even harm you. Ever felt deathly afraid to get close to someone? This fear doesn't make your desire to be close go away. It just puts large objects in the way for you to trip over. It gives you a ton of reasons why you can't get close, taking your mind deeper into fear and shutting you down further from the possibility of intimacy.

Your world gets smaller every time these reasons go unchallenged; you become a disciple to your own personal gospel of BS. To be able to get close requires courage, vulnerability, and openness. It means you walk right into the unknown, the uncontrollable, and the uncomfortable. There is no such thing as true protection emotionally, no matter what your mind says—so why can't you take the leap? Well, your reasons seem uber-valid. Staying safe feels comfortable, even if it is dissatisfying.

To change to a bigger perspective means believing that you can say yes to what has meaning for you and no to suffering for no valid reason. If other people come before you when you choose for their benefit and against your own, then I suggest you stop for a moment and become very aware of why you believe your sacrifice is beneficial to them. Be aware of what you are actually sacrificing. Be aware of what you expect in return. Do not lie to yourself. Do not assume you know what is going on inside someone when you do not. Do not talk yourself into this action out of fear of disappointing someone. You will just hate yourself, and you might be laying something on them that they want no part of.

People aren't made happy by our sacrifices; they are made happy by their own choice to be happy. Thinking you have the power to control their happiness by selling yourself to handcuffs is a fallacy. Your world will continue to shrink into one of bitterness with these types of sacrifices, and that's about as fun as skinny-dipping in the Arctic.

Getting close to what you fear is not for the faint of heart; in fact, you must build that heart muscle. Emotional resilience is a big part of the heart muscle. Many of us fear we don't have emotional resilience. We fear we won't survive our own feelings. Fear keeps things murky. It's hard to know exactly how feelings will kill us, but to be on the safe side, we choose the situation we know rather than the unknown.

The key to building the heart muscle is to approach your emotions slowly and stay as present as you can in the moment, especially when you're about to say no to someone you usually drop everything for. You might feel a mixture of guilt, elation, second-guessing, doubt, and peace. It's okay. It gets easier the more you do it. After a while it won't feel that you are doing things against others when you put your own needs first. In fact, over time, you will have more compassion and kindness as you turn someone down. Remember that all your actions *for you* rather than *against you* build up that heart and create emotional resilience. Go toward it. This is new for most people—it will feel odd.

As children, we learned that it's not okay to be in favor of ourselves, but rather that we should conform to societal standards, like "Don't be a starving artist!" or "What do you mean you want to drop out of college?" Be aware of your propensity to go against yourself. Pay attention to how moving slowly allows you to be at a pace to notice what you normally skim right over in your words and actions.

Going toward your fear, feeling your feelings as you take actions, brings you closer to the ability to live from an unlimited state of possibility. As you make movement, you will notice yourself dropping your limited ideas of what you can or cannot do. Always stay in connection with your feelings as you forge ahead on the road to becoming your own best friend. This is how you will grow happier and become more connected to yourself.

SHAME DENIES YOU OF YES

Shame is a universal emotion that comes alive from our own personal stories about our value and what we deserve. Giving yourself permission to do what you truly want is difficult when you believe your own story about shame. Sometimes you avoid making a choice that will induce shame, to avoid awakening those painful personal stories. Skipping over shame, or somehow saying yes to yourself with conditions, might keep the sleeping giant of shame asleep, temporarily. But by creating conditions—like "I can say yes only if the sun sets at 5:01 today and I win the lottery"—you still aren't choosing you. If shame is a factor, you will continue to choose against yourself.

Shame says, "I do not deserve—I am without value—I did things wrong, so I pay a penance or deny myself." Long ago, you developed stories of right versus wrong; good versus evil. Many of us have spent our lives striving to remain on what we perceive as the good side, even if the cost is denying ourselves the pursuit of our own passions. It's funny that trying to stay on the good side doesn't guarantee you won't slip and fall into doing something to upset someone's apple cart, or your own. What do you do then? Backtrack, apologize, avoid, deny? None of those behaviors supports saying yes to yourself. "Maybe someday" stories might come up—as though, if you can work through life correctly and finally not be a shame-producing being, you'll be allowed to sit at the adult table.

It is impossible to wait until shame has been emptied out of you to finally feel that you deserve to say yes to yourself. What if Marilyn wanted to do stand-up comedy, because she felt she was funny, but she feared failing miserably? Even though she loved the idea, the prospect of public failure seemed too scary—if nobody laughed, she didn't think she'd be able to stand the shame. So, she came up with excuses not to try.

At other times, shame keeps you feeling bad about yourself—you can feel as if you cannot ever be okay. I did drugs when I was younger, and for years I beat myself up and felt less deserving than others who'd never taken that route. I had a hard time choosing to honor my feelings; I did not know how. I waited for guaranteed approval before I took some chances on myself. And of course, there is no such thing.

This went back to my relationship with my parents, where for years I felt guilty for choosing my feelings. There were no specific incidents around not honoring myself. I spoke to my mother regularly. I'd ask how she was, and usually the answer was "same old, same old." She would ask about me and, depending on what year it was, I could launch into venting about work, or struggle to find a topic. I didn't know what to talk about because sooner or later, she would remind me that all I talked about was myself. Nothing seemed safe. I knew that talking about my life and myself would be a problem sooner or later, but I wasn't sure what else to do. I would always think I was doing the right thing by sharing, but then things would go sideways, and there my father or mother would go, telling me negative things about myself. For years, I felt lost without a map. I could not please them. In fact, that realization was the lightbulb moment—that's when I understood that no matter what I did, I wasn't a mind reader, and the circumstances were already set up for me to bite the dust. But even once I had that knowledge, my choices were limited. For a long time, it left me unsure whether I was choosing for me or against me when I communicated regularly with my parents.

As I grew emotionally, it became very clear that I would have to make different choices to deal with the feelings of shame when it came to my interactions with them and the general guilt and shame around not being a good enough daughter.

My shame was deep. It went back to being a kid who was very sensitive to what others said. My parents said things to me that impacted me deeply, making me feel like I was unworthy. These exchanges would leave me feeling as though I should curl up in a ball and die. I was shamed for being myself—right or wrong, it was what happened. I never felt entitled to my feelings. I was told that they were wrong, and to stop feeling that way. I felt that I should not believe my feelings. This seemed so strange, but it had to be true—why would they say that my feelings were wrong it if it wasn't true? This disconnect between what I felt inside and what I was being told was confusing and painful. When I grew up to be an adult, whenever things came up that created shame, it brought those old feelings, too. It limited my choices. It was funny. My parents often said to me as an adult, "Why do you only remember the negative parts of your childhood?" I did remember other things, but in trying to unravel my shame and distance from my feelings, the negative stuff really was front and center.

It was a painful feeling of humiliation or distress. Like so many others, when I felt shame, the last thing I wanted to do was admit it, to myself or others. And so, with my parents, complying with expectations was the only way I could keep my shame at bay. As an adult, I would inevitably be triggered by something one of them said or did, and all hell would break loose. I wanted to choose me, but I didn't know how to do that.

I finally came to choosing myself when my parents decided not to attend my wedding. It wasn't just the fact that they didn't come—it was the reasons they gave, their treatment of me, the things they said to others, and the realization that no matter what I did, it was always going to be that way. I am sure my parents love me, and that to them, the motivation for not coming felt justified.

I took responsibility for having reacted in pain to their decision not to come to my wedding, but I absolutely refused to feel that their actions, words, or choices were my responsibility, especially in the aftermath of my nuptials. Whew! That was hard.

After that, I began to notice that the more I took responsibility for everything I said and did, the less shame drove my actions. Choosing myself set me free. I no longer had to be beaten over the head with old voices telling me I was bad. It became clear how shame, for years, had pushed or pulled me to make choices that had nothing to do with my own well-being.

I'm not blaming my parents, by the way. You do not choose you when you blame someone else for how you feel. Yes, people impact you, as my parents impacted me. But they were just doing what worked for them, from their perspective. I had to start doing what worked for me. I learned that by trying too hard, I might as well have not tried at all. I had hoped that at some point I would be good enough to be given the opportunity to lose all the shame and then choose myself. But it worked the other way around: first I chose myself, then I worked through my shame and let it go.

How can you possibly choose yourself when you feel like you are wrong or could fail? Well, you just do it. Go through all the feelings associated with it. Allow every ounce of shame and cringe that comes with the feelings. And you might as well get used to feeling wrong. It's a feeling, not a life sentence. It's not going to kill you; it will pass.

When you avoid shame, it grows. When you're able to recognize shame as a product of your story rather than a universal right or wrong, it becomes easier to break it apart.

DOOMED TO STRUGGLE; HOW DO I STOP?

Life does life. You have a choice. You do not have to struggle with it. You can choose you. You do have to accept that life does whatever it is going to do whether you fight it or not.

In other words, you must learn acceptance if you want to be happy. Acceptance just means saying *"Yes, there is oxygen* (acceptance)," rather than "No, there is no oxygen" (resistance). It may sound ludicrous, but that's how ludicrous it is when we fight life. We sometimes believe that if we fight to get what we want then we can say yes to ourselves, but that doesn't work, either. The prize is always outside your control. You might feel that you've chosen yourself by striving for and achieving certain goals, but that feeling is temporary. There's no restfulness to it; you will go back to believing you must do more.

A client of mine wrote about acceptance: "This morning, I decided that I can't wait… to start living life, or to start loving someone, or wait until I reach nirvana in order to begin living. I decided to do it right now. Even though I feel somewhat defeated, I still loved the idea of the puppy with the baby and the man. And I still enjoyed talking to the lady beside me telling the story about the funny old ladies on the metro. I dressed up to go to a memorial service and felt thankful that I am alive and vibrant. I'm surrounding myself with color and beauty and plant life. I still feel lonely, incomplete, and less than. But I also feel happy and relaxed and hopeful. Today I'm going to be accepting of all that I am."

Life doing life means you can stop the struggle against it. The minute you get that you do not have to struggle (yeah, yeah, you say it all the time, but to practice it is a different story), you learn what ease truly is. I used to force things to happen all the time. Years ago, I had a business. I met someone in the animation industry and immediately decided I needed to work for him. I shut my business down and forced the door open with him. By doing this, I did not choose me. When I started there, I realized my mistake because of the position I was given. Now granted, he created a position for me, and I was so eager to prove myself that I would've mopped the bathroom floors. But my desire to change what I was doing and at the same time force my way into an industry that I thought was my destiny would've been easier had I allowed life to do life. If I had taken the time to connect to myself, there could have been a whole different outcome.

Instead I struggled a great deal—it took a long time for me to choose myself, and by the time I did it, I was deflated and defeated. My foray into the field would make for a movie scenario. But living through it, I really had to take a look at how I was full of integrity with others, but dishonest with myself. I sold myself a story about how amazing people were—people that I put on a pedestal, trusting they would never do anything bad. But they were human. And lots of bad things happened, where I struggled. I so desperately wanted this fantasy to come true; I wanted happiness that I thought would come through my career in animation. I had gotten what I supposedly wanted, but it ended up being a handful of crap—an outcome that, had I not been forcing things, I would have seen in reality. I was still years away from understanding how I had created an unnecessary struggle in my quest for my fantasy fulfillment. Struggles like this are not the same as choosing yourself easily.

What about you? Have you been in a struggle that is going nowhere? What is your strategy to win so you get to finally say yes to yourself? If you're trying to push life, force your will upon it, now is the time to get deeper with yourself and learn why. You need to know what it is you fear you cannot have without a struggle.

Many people believe in lassoing life or tethering it to what feels comfortable to them, so they can be happy. But struggle is not a state of happiness. It is not in alignment with taking care of yourself. If anything, it keeps you running in circles toward something that will end up being a constant reminder that you felt you did not deserve to choose you. You'll continue to believe you're undeserving, and you'll keep proving it to yourself by ignoring your own experience and pushing forward toward unexamined goals.

WAITING FOR THE PAYOFF

Do you have an underlying belief that life owes you? Many people do. At some point, the hope is that you will have collected enough brownie points and life will suddenly offer you the big jackpot! You might even believe that life will become easy at that point, so you can sit back and "finally" be happy. Maybe you feel you have suffered long and hard, and that's just what you had to do for the big payoff.

What does life owe you? Have you ever stopped, sat down, closed your eyes, and asked the question, "What am I fighting for?" then dug deeper, connected to your feelings, and come to see the "yes" it will give you? Sometimes we believe life owes us because we learned this as children. We learned if we do the "right thing," it is supposed to reward us. But whether any payoff comes or not, you will never be able to get back the part of yourself that you sacrificed to get there. Striving for brownie points will have turned you into somebody you don't even want to know.

It is important to see how this thought process works against us, and to understand that life's rewards come without us fighting for them.

If you still believe you're entitled, you need to ask deeper questions. First, why? Why would you believe that life owes you? Second, even if life paid off exactly how you wanted it to, how do you know that it would feel any different from the way it feels now? Your feelings do not change because there is a payoff in life. Sure, at first you might be excited, but as this gift becomes your new reality, it will wear off. Third, can you allow life to do what it does and make choices that speak to your happiness right now?

This is a choice you may not be prepared to make. It might seem that sacrifice and struggle are just the way you are supposed to do things. Like chores as a kid; you worked for your quarter or dollar. If you didn't mow the lawn or babysit, you were told you did not deserve your own money. After a while it seems there is a price attached to saying yes to yourself. But that's just one model of reality.

In a reality of ease and happiness, it doesn't actually work that way. You just choose you and allow everything around you to choose as well.

ACCEPTANCE

Acceptance is about letting go and saying, "Okay, life is doing whatever it does." This allows you to stop running in circles, going against yourself, and depleting yourself of your life energy.

It's time to stop going against yourself and choose you, no matter what life is throwing your way. Be courageous. There's no strategy to calculate. Just release that tight grip and allow life to do its thing!

You are the boss of your life, but not of life. You do not get to stand in front of a wall and say, "That's not there," then walk through it without injuring yourself.

Acceptance doesn't mean you love it or you like it, it means you accept that it exists. It is what it is. You have to acknowledge the wall exists and if you still choose to walk through it, you know you will not come out unscathed. But ask yourself, "How does this help me, walking through the wall? What do I receive that is in alignment with my truth and my happiness; how am I taking care of me?" The wall is the wall—it is not something to be struggled against or resisted. Be in reality. The one right here and now. If you don't, the same struggle will continue.

In stopping your struggle with life, guess what happens? You stop distracting yourself from truly living. You are immediately choosing you.

Remember I spoke about the locus of control? When life controls your mood, your choices, and how you see things, you will stay in struggle. Digging deeper may show you that what you thought would "fix" your life may not have anything to do with who you are and what is meaningful. It's so much better to make the authentic choice of alignment with yourself, because the payoff is so much sweeter.

It's not about fixing your life. The more you choose you, the more things will self-correct that you previously could not accept. You may have been asking for a long time for specific circumstances to be true, but not know why. You've been distracted, analyzing battle plans against life. When you stop the battle, you set yourself free from its grip. You start living like you mean it. If you stop forcing life into a corner, you will be surprised by all the abundance it has to give to you.

Struggle is a choice. Stop choosing to hurt yourself and start to build internal value. Your feelings will start to matter because someone cares about them. That someone is you. Life will shift toward you in a much more friendly way, not as an opponent, and you will be ready to create.

NOW STOP GOING AGAINST YOURSELF AS A VICTIM/MARTYR

To choose yourself, look at why you are afraid to take care of you. What do you fear? Maybe you're stuck on the drama triangle. Maybe you're used to dropping what you do for yourself and choosing the desire of another, to your detriment. Maybe you find it easier to say no to something you have always wanted to do, coming up with a million excuses as to why you can't. Maybe you're just comfortable with the internal struggle you have known your entire life. It's what has driven you. Where would you be without it? You might have no idea what it would feel like to love yourself enough to stop going against yourself.

First, rest assured that you can do it. But you have to really have the courage to stand up and feel. To become responsible for your choices, you have to own your stuff. You have to give up "going along to get along." You have to give up hope that you will finally somehow *earn* the right to choose yourself. You were born with that right. What you have to do now is *unlearn* all the things that have stopped you from exercising it.

As you learn to do this, you will discover that choosing yourself is where you learn to trust yourself. Through experience, you start to find what your true needs are and respond to them.

EXERCISE: Stop Playing Victim

Even if you currently believe you choose yourself without the blink of an eye, there may still be times where it is hard to put yourself first. Grab your journal and find a quiet space for 30 to 45. It is important to use the tools you learned in Chapter 3 on feeling your real feelings as you complete this exercise.

1. Look back on yesterday (or choose a day you have a solid memory of). Notice if there was any time where you chose *no* instead of *yes* to something you really wanted (I am not talking about buying that four-hundred-thousand-dollar car or another impossible dream. I'm talking about something you could have said yes to, but didn't.) What did it feel like to say no in this instance? Feel your feelings and then describe them, to the best of your ability, in your journal.

2. As you think about your past few days or weeks, start to notice how often you do this. Does it seem like there's a recurring pattern of choosing to go against yourself in everyday life?

3. Now lean into your observations, doing the body scan from Chapter 3. Pay attention to the internal struggle—what does it feel like? What is it distracting you from?

4. When you review your notes and see how you've chosen to stay stuck, listen and feel the physical sensations—it feels bad, doesn't it? What do you do with those bad feelings? Do you compartmentalize and shove them down more, hoping they will go away? Try giving them some space now, by writing them down or saying them out loud.

5. What will happen if you say yes to yourself for something you really want? What is your greatest fear? What is the worst thing that could happen? Breathe and imagine yourself in that situation. Let your feelings arise. Stay with them and feel for the answers, then allow them to move through you.

6. Can you commit to a risk (make sure you feel it emotionally) and say yes? If so, what does the risk look like? An example would be to stop blaming your boss for what he or she does and instead take responsibility for your own actions, including the fact that you really do not want to work there. You want to start your own business creating natural soap and toiletries. And admitting the truth: that it is not about looking for reasons blamed on others, but that stating your desire or taking a step forward will be an emotionally risky action.

7. Once you have a clear idea about what is happening inside of you, you can challenge your old story by taking the step of sticking with a commitment for yourself. What would taking a step out of your norm be? How, specifically, will you stop saying yes when you mean no? (Example: I am going to stop running myself ragged for my friend Alice. The next time Alice calls with another dilemma, such as needing a ride home from dinner and I'm already tucked into bed, I will say, "I am sorry to hear that, Alice, such a bummer! I would love to help you out, but I can't. If you need a suggestion for a car service, let me know. Otherwise I hope you have a good night.")

Saying no to someone you've been saying yes to isn't just a favor you're doing yourself. Allowing this person to be responsible for their own choices is doing them a big favor, too. Now, you may feel guilty or uncomfortable, but just sit with your feelings and they will become less intense. Imagine what you'd have felt like if you'd jumped out of bed to fix things for Alice. You would have been full of resentment and anger—wondering when you're going to matter enough to be first in your life. You would make yourself a victim on the drama triangle.

When you value yourself by taking care of yourself in this way, no matter how small the step, it is a game changer. You might temporarily feel a bit out of sorts, but that's okay! You are allowed to prioritize yourself. You are learning that you matter!

And if, once in a while, you find yourself giving in to the Alices in your life, be honest with yourself about what you're doing. Do not make excuses or sweep it away. Do it if you must, but at the same time, look for where you are afraid in this relationship, somewhere you feel you may suffer a loss, or something that has you choosing to go against yourself. Consider whether you're just used to being on the drama triangle with Alice, or if your fear of disappointing her runs deeper.

There will come a time when you realize that you haven't chosen someone else over yourself for a long time, and you will be able to see what an effect choosing yourself has had on your life and the lives of the people you care about.

CHAPTER 9

Step 6—Stop Assuming and Personalizing

The pattern of assuming and personalizing means you never learned it was okay to rely on your own innate thoughts, feelings, actions, or words. In this step, you dig deep to where the original insecurity comes from by questioning the emotional purpose of the assumptions you make about others. You learn to speak your truth without blame, to ask questions without fear, and to be vulnerable without shame.

STORIES IN YOUR HEAD THAT KEEP YOU STUCK

An assumption is what you come up with when you do not know the truth but think you do. You make assumptions based on what you believe other people are thinking without any evidence to support this idea. Your assumptions are based on circumstances that you identify through your own perception of the world and your place in it. Assumptions coordinate well with personalizing. Making assumptions was once my go-to strategy. I believed that whatever people did was because of me, and that my impact was always negative. I never considered the idea that I might leave a positive mark on someone else's life.

Personalizing meant I took everything personally. I thought that what other people said or did had meaning about me in a negative way. All this assuming and personalizing meant that I also did a lot of predicting. Often, I found out how far off I really was in my assumptions and personalization.

These are painful behaviors. Whether I was reading someone's mind without any actual knowledge of what was going on in there or believing that whatever they were doing was because of me—it was painful. For years, everything in my life was about other people and what they thought. Of course, I fought that idea for a long time: "Nah, I don't care what anyone thinks of me!" But when I was honest with myself, I saw that it was my entire focus. Living my life this way was a 1,000 percent distraction from me. I really had no sense of myself. I was too busy trying to preempt any unforeseeable issues from happening.

One of my deepest dreads was to be misunderstood. So many of us work very hard to avoid this. If I could figure out what you were thinking, then I could act accordingly, and I would be understood. When I was misunderstood, I took it personally. I figured my fatal flaw had been figured out. I did a lot of reconnaissance to keep things under control. I worked so hard to be understood that I couldn't let it fall apart. It was critical for me to only do things others would like and appreciate; to talk them into understanding me and my motivation so

Overcoming Insecure Attachment

they would know I would never to anything to purposely upset them. It was like living as a cardboard cutout of myself!

Everyday assumptions are a part of our lives. Anywhere the words "always," "never," "nothing," "everyone," or "everything" appear, there's an assumption: "I am always late for work." "He is always in a bad mood." "Everyone is against me." "Nothing ever works out for me." And so on. Unfortunately, these assumptions can set you up for the exact circumstances you don't want. Remember, when you say these things to yourself you start reacting to them, and this reaction is what creates your next words and actions. If you didn't believe they were true, you would set up entirely different circumstances.

But for many, it seems far more important to be right about what they assume. It's painful to live this way, but it is a pattern. If you assume and it comes true, you feel validated, even if it is something you would prefer didn't happen.

Making assumptions does not work as a way to control other people. You may believe that performing acrobatics in response to a story you have told yourself about what you think someone else is thinking is controlling the situation. It's not. The only thing it controls is you. In fact, it makes you act in ways that aren't clear.

Fear is the driver, but what is the underlying cause of your motivating fear? Look at your assumption. You are reacting to it. Why? This story in your head is not true. Even if you guess right about someone's thoughts and feelings, then what? What is your goal? For them to like you? To convince them you are worthy to be their friend, supplier, client, or colleague? To have them leave? Look at your negative beliefs. They are a motivator in creating assumptions. They need to be proven true; your assumptions give you evidence of their truth.

Assumptions keep you repeating a lot of the same behaviors over and over. Even if new people or situations show up in your life, you apply your old pattern of making assumptions about them. Pay attention— you will see it happening—it's pretty interesting when you are aware of how this undermines you. There is no emotional freedom in assuming. In trying to avoid being misunderstood or abandoned, you make no forward movement, just circular. This circle says you need others to be captivated by your performance. Otherwise, who would you be?

TALL TALES, ANYONE?

You've heard there are always two sides to a story. Actually, there are as many sides as there are people involved because stories are based on perspectives. When you build a case against someone, you are sticking to your story. Your version of reality is based on your beliefs and assumptions born from those beliefs. Nevertheless, you may believe you are right or better because that's what your story demands.

But right and wrong, better and worse are subjective, and they will get you absolutely nothing—except an illusion. Even though stories are about other people, you can be immersed in them and think they are reality. The problem is that these are the stories you live off when you make your decisions in life. And making decisions based on stories will restrict your possibilities.

Any story restricts your possibilities because you are attached to only one outcome. You have told yourself the same story over and over on autopilot: who you think you are and who you must be for other people. You might even believe you have a crystal ball on how your day will unfold, but it's all based on your assumptions. This story colors your perception of everything. When you live from this story, you have certain judgments (right, wrong, etc.) and patterns to support it. You don't think about how your words and actions affect other people, because you're just following your usual script.

It's hard to have awareness about some of these stories since they feel so real, and you can surely find evidence to their truth somewhere. You often have no idea you're living inside a story. The only way to become aware that it's a story is if someone calls you out on it, making you question its validity, or if you have a reaction to it that wakes you up!

As you grow your self-awareness, you start to realize that what you think is reality is actually just the same old story replaying itself. You realize that your assumptions are BS, and that the evidence you claim supports them is cherry-picked from events outside of you. You conclude that these stories are rather toxic. They create the opposite of what you say you want for yourself.

Once you see that you're working from a story, ask yourself why you need it. Does it contribute to your survival, or to your happiness? Who would you be without the story? One is safe and known, the other unsafe and unknown. What would it be like to let go of your story and get closer to the real you?

Let's say you want your partner to fit into the story of how you want your life to be. And they accommodate you: whatever house you want to buy, however you want to decorate it, wherever you want to go for dinner; whatever you want, you get.

You always have your way, until one day your partner asserts him/herself and doesn't go along with the program. This throws you into a tizzy, because things *can't* be any other way. Your assumption is that they only love you if they are doing for you. So, they must not love you! You assume this story and you react to it; you are upset and feel rejected. Your partner has no clue what your issue is—they are just tired of always giving in to your way. You don't know what to do with yourself now that he/she suddenly has a desire to do something different.

Now you have a choice: either be in a battle with them or accept that they're going to do what they're going to do. True acceptance and peace mean changing your story.

You can challenge your stories: what if they aren't true? Answering that question could change your life, because it will open up a whole new way of seeing things—things you can't currently see in your version of reality.

But you say, "Wait! He/she is an asshole! Poor me, I have a right to be angry. I'm right, they are wrong. And I need to be right." Perhaps you fear people will walk all over you.

Angry stories are a way of staying stuck. You can keep choosing the path of being self-righteous, or you can break down your assumptions and see that they carry no weight. The more you allow reality to just be what it is and stop trying to fit it into your stories, the happier you will be.

WHAT'S WRONG WITH ME?

Always trying to prove you are good enough means that you often take the comments and/or actions of others personally. It may have nothing to do with their intention, but if you feel like they are judging you, you will personalize, internalize, and use the supposed judgment to confirm your belief that you're not good enough and everything you do is wrong.

I had a client who was an art instructor. She believed people didn't think she was good enough, smart enough, or cool enough to be a real artist. This issue rose to a head any time she compared herself to her coworkers—her peers. She personalized, thinking that if someone was or was not smiling, it must be because of something she'd done. She also took it personally when her class attendance went down, even if it had nothing to do with her.

Then one day, a woman in one of her painting classes came up to her and said, "I really haven't learned a good technique here. I think it is because you are not a patient teacher." My client was mortified, but inside her head, she was saying to herself, "I knew it! I knew I sucked! And now I should just quit!" These thoughts fed right into her assumptions about herself—the belief that she wasn't good enough.

Whether this comment from a student had any merit is beside the point. The problem was that my client based her whole self-worth on what others thought of her. Even if it was only one other person. Now she had proof that her assumption was correct.

People have their own issues and often project their fears onto others. It goes both ways, because you do the same thing. When someone triggers you it's not about them, it's about you, but it can be hard to see that. It is not on purpose; they do not know your emotional baggage, and even if they did, they have their own.

If someone says something judgmental about you, it doesn't mean you're the problem. It's their problem, their perception, and their belief. It doesn't belong to you.

I received an email from someone I thought was a friend about owing her something. I felt sad for her, because I realized it was her fear that caused her to write to me in the tone she did. How she saw me and what she was accusing me of had nothing to do with me; it was all her assumption. In the old days, getting this email would've spun me out. I would've taken it personally. In this case, it was clear that the person she wrote to wasn't me, it was her perception of me through the fearful lens by which she viewed her reality. Big difference.

Another friend helped me move. She had a slight meltdown because so much was unfinished in our house with the remodel. I was already stressed, and that added to it. While I didn't overreact as I would've in the past, it made me question whether I was seeing the situation clearly, or if I was delusional. I had to work hard to stop personalizing her fear and discomfort. But I knew it wasn't mine. I was able to skip right out of that quagmire once I really felt that it was not my problem.

Often, when personalizing, you may be in a state of reaction. You might shut down or fight back to defend yourself. It may not be anything someone is saying or doing, either—you may personalize based on your assumption about how they feel.

Personalizing leads to jumping into boiling water without checking the temperature. Even when someone has criticized you, you may want to look for the truth without beating yourself up. If criticism triggers you, it is a sign that something inside you is being pushed. If the other person has something valuable to say, it can change things around for you to listen without taking it personally.

With my friend who was freaked out about our house, instead of shutting down, I opened up to her about how her comments triggered my fears. I didn't blame her, and it became a funny event between us. Luckily, in being open and talking it through, I was able to see that some of her input *was* valuable. She cared about me, and not only was I able to see that, but I was able to feel grateful.

Ever need to call customer service? Do you get annoyed and think they are deliberately trying to ruin your day? Thirty minutes of your life disappears while waiting to speak to a computer. As you wait, you get more and more pissed. You are finally rerouted to a person, and by then you want to reach through the phone and rip their head off. You are personalizing this whole experience, but it's not about you. It's how this company runs their business. The employee you want to harm has little to do with your frustration. If you could sit back and feel your rage, what would it tell you? What is it you believe about being put through this three-ring circus?

What if you could instead stay compassionate with the person doing his or her job? You would then have the emotional freedom to not judge the situation from a place of pain. Taking people personally rarely helps anyone. But being aware when you catch yourself doing it *is* helpful.

SELF-REFLECTION IN THE MIRROR OF LIFE

There is an opportunity to see yourself by seeing other people. You may have heard the expression, "When you point your finger at someone, accusing them of wrongdoing, the rest of your fingers point back at you." There is truth in this statement, but it goes further. People may not exhibit the exact same traits as you, but they may share the same negative belief about themselves.

Let's say your partner is jealous. They're always asking to see your phone or even sneaking looks at it when you're in the shower. Fights ensue. It's the same ugly conversation, different day. He is jealous, but it's more than that. He has been cheated on in the past. His self-worth when he was cheated on wasn't great, and now it is even lower.

But before we get too far in making him wrong or assuming things about him, let's add that your own self-worth matches his. Who you choose to be with mirrors what you think of yourself. If he exhibits characteristics of low self-worth and even admits to it, perhaps you need to look at your own self-worth. Taking the reflection of another person and applying it inward is far healthier than assuming and personalizing. In fact, making the trip inward lets you disconnect from the assuming and personalizing, because the journey is now about you and not about others. Instead of judging and strategizing based on your assumption, it lets you become aware of and address something in yourself to create a change. If you are caught up in assuming something about your best friend, take a step back. Instead of assuming, get to the core of why you make up a story.

Perhaps you assume your friend only wants to hang out with you when she has time. If you don't hear from her, you assume she is busy. You do not reach out because you assume she doesn't want to talk or hang out. Weeks might go by. Finally, she reaches out to you and says, "Hey there! I haven't heard from you in a while, is everything okay? I would've reached out sooner but I get the idea you don't really want to hang out or talk, because I never hear from you." You are dumbstruck, because this reflects your own assumptions perfectly.

What does this tell you, besides the fact that you both assume a lot and don't take a lot of action toward connecting? It might show you that you don't think very much of yourself. You might see that you feel you are someone to be tolerated, rather than cared about. You might see how your lack of value is reflected to you by your friend, who has the same issue. This could help you to do something about it, rather than waiting for others to show you your value.

Now look at your assumptions about yourself. Do you assume you're a lover, not a fighter? If so, what do you do and say to support that image? Maybe you do nothing, and others assume you're a fighter because you seem rather combative. If others assume incorrectly about you, and even you assume incorrectly about yourself, who could ever assume correctly? When you discover someone's assuming something about who you are, take the time to reflect on it. Look at why you come off as a fighter. What are you protecting about yourself?

What others assume is not the truth, but you are not showing your truth, either. When you are totally matching what you do, say, and believe, you are in alignment with yourself—you feel great! It is the trifecta! And whether people make assumptions about you or not is unimportant.

When what you say, do, and believe don't align, you look to others for clues about yourself, assuming and personalizing. I guarantee you do not feel "good enough." In opposition to your truth, you are acting based on what you assume about others, rather than what you really know to be true about yourself. You are focusing on what you assume they want or think, instead of being who you really are.

Bring the reflection back to you. Use it to see yourself clearly. You might see a characteristic in your friend that says he is overly competitive. He always wants to challenge you to a game. You assume he's a sore loser, because he usually stops talking and shuts down by the end of the game. You don't think you're overly competitive, although when you are losing you get a sinking feeling inside. You start assuming that he is jealous of you. Meanwhile, you assume that you're a good sport and wish nothing but the best for your buddy.

This scenario could be true—your friend may be more insecure than you are when playing games—but how do you know? Are you aware of your own feelings, not just the story in your head that says your behavior is okay? You may want to ask yourself why you need to assume you are good and your friend has the issue. Why don't you ask him how he feels when he loses? You could say that it appears he is not okay with losing, but you don't want to assume, so you're asking. Meanwhile, you need to look at why you assume that you're better than him, and think that he's the one with an issue.

When we judge—and assuming is a type of judgment—we are acting out of a need to feel superior. How does it serve your self-perception to take his negative behavior and create a story that makes you the better person?

COMMON AREAS FOR ASSUMING

Here's a short list of some areas to look at as you prepare to focus on finding an assumption that causes you pain.

- Assuming scarcity exists in your life. You look around the room and say, "Well, I guess this is it. This is how it always has been, or always will be," or "I'm alone, because no one is physically here," or "I don't have _____ because I never do; it will never change," or "S/he is the best I'll ever have, so I'd better just get used to it."

- Assuming you know what others think of you.

- Assuming you know all possible outcomes to any situation.

- Assuming your intellect has the solution to problems that were created emotionally (and these are the same old solutions, too).

- Assuming things that delude your into remaining in a false sense of safety.

- Assuming you know what someone else is doing. (Even thinking you'll outsmart 'em.)

- Assuming you're right and someone else is wrong.

- Personalizing, which means victimization (you can live out the whole drama triangle in your mind).

- Personalizing, which means you interpret others' words and actions to be because of, or about, you.

COMMON ASSUMPTIONS

- I will always be alone; I've been alone 10 years and haven't gone on a date in three years. No one ever asks me out.

- I'll never get a raise; I am afraid to ask, I couldn't handle being turned down.

- I'm always broke and will never get my head above water; it's been this way since I was on my own.

- I have to "do" something in order to receive love; just being me isn't enough. I'm always cooking, cleaning, and doing errands for my partner.

- If I commit to this person/job/life, I may miss out on something better. It seems I always choose and find out 10 minutes later I should've waited.

- I work my ass off in every relationship and always end up being the bad guy or gal. My partner blames me for everything—no matter what, I end up here.

NOW STOP ASSUMING AND PERSONALIZING

When you assume and personalize you have little understanding about your own contribution toward why your life looks the way it does. You may feel confused or puzzled about why you cannot seem to have better circumstances, because you do not connect to how your assumptions and personalizing match up to your negative beliefs. Well, let's take steps to change that.

The following exercise gets to the core beliefs that drive your assumptions. You can do this exercise over and over again, with every assumption you own. You want to illuminate your core beliefs, so you know what drives the bus of your life. You want to stop assuming and letting unconscious actions create havoc.

EXERCISE: Name Your Assumption and Understand Why You Personalize

Grab your journal and carve out 45 to 60 minutes of time in a quiet space. This is an eight-step exercise. Pay attention to your feelings as you answer the questions.

As you do this exercise, keep in mind that the goal is self-empowerment, compassion, and confidence, which lead to a feeling of emotional freedom. It's incremental. Do these consistently, but at your own pace. This exercise requires taking your time to allow it to sink in emotionally. Once you are able to fully complete a step, move onto the next one. These build off each other, taking you deeper each time, so don't rush it.

To start this exercise, think about an area in your life you want to improve, change, or get unstuck in. You might think of a person whose words and actions in this area you take personally. You will know you've hit on a good area if you immediately notice a physical reaction when you think about it. Perhaps your stomach tightens, your chest feels heavy, or you clench your jaw or tighten elsewhere in your body—just notice the reaction.

Now notice how you feel about your thoughts. See if you feel imprisoned by the situation or anxious to be free of it. Look for where you think your assumptions may play a major role in your dissatisfaction. Also pay attention to how personalizing the actions and words of others makes you feel bad. These areas may include intimate relationships, friendships, professional relationships, goals/life direction, handling pain or difficult emotions, commitment, etc.

Perhaps you feel, "I can't seem to have a healthy relationship, but I really want one. No matter what, all my efforts seem in vain—so why try?" This is a place where more than one story exists. You can also see where you personalize: "My boyfriend never mentions getting married, and that makes me feel bad."

Sit for a moment with it and get clearer about what it is and how it feels inside you. You have chosen this story or stories and will use it to take you through the steps of the exercise. If there is more than one area, that's fine—just do one at a time. You can repeat this exercise for each area you want to improve. It is important to use the tools you learned in Chapter 3 on feeling your real feelings.

STEP 1—NAME YOUR MAIN ASSUMPTION

Focus on the feelings related to the area you named. Is there one overarching assumption that replays in your head? (If it helps, review Common Assumptions on page 193.)

More will naturally follow, as from one assumption several more are born. Write your main assumption down in your journal.

When you mull over your assumption, take notice of what exactly you assume. In other words, if you say you're always broke, what is it really saying—is it speaking to your career, your finances, or your inability to stop spending frivolously?

In naming an assumption, you want to be specific. People have a tendency to make their assumptions too general, and it can become overwhelming to dig deeply with clarity.

If possible, once you believe you have your assumption in focus, spend time looking at this assumption daily, seeing how it pops up in different circumstances. It will be very evident, and you may be surprised at all the places this assumption lives in your life.

Keep the assumption in your field of awareness and write it in your journal, using the words, "My main assumption is . . ."

List things you notice about the assumption, such as the situations it shows up in, the time of day, how you are feeling about yourself, and other events going on that may or may not have anything to do with you.

STEP 2—IDENTIFY THE EMOTIONS ATTACHED TO THE ASSUMPTION

As you go through your days, watch your repetitive assumption popping up in your thoughts—it should be clear enough by now that you will have a hard time ignoring it.

The next step comes when you are in the heat of the moment, reacting to this assumption or to a situation that has been created from it. For example, let's say you have an assumption that you can't get a date. Personalizing it would mean that even if you were on a dating site, a person not getting back to you says there is something wrong with you. Your assumption has shown you that you have this idea every Friday night, when you believe everyone else is out on a date. You also notice that you do nothing to change the situation. In fact, you think because you can't get a date, you shouldn't even try. So you do not bother. Now your best friend calls to tell you she is getting married.

You need to stop your reaction (if you aren't hysterical) and find the emotion attached to the physical feeling of reaction inside you, then allow yourself to feel into it, wherever it is located in your body. This is the same action as described in the chapter on feeling your feelings by working with triggers.

If you look closely, you will find ongoing pain and/or difficulty. You need to name it. What is the emotion attached to your assumption (e.g., loneliness, happiness, sadness, distrust, safety, etc.)? List them in your journal, using the words, "Emotions attached to my assumption are..."

STEP 3—GET SPECIFIC

Please continue here only after you have really spent time getting clear on your main assumption and the emotions driving it around a particular area of your life.

Now let's take it deeper and get specific about *why* the feelings you named are connected to the assumption. Are the feelings tied into hope or fear that the assumption will be proven true, or conversely, that it will be disproved? Is it the outcome your emotions are tied up in, or is it the story itself?

For example, let's say you discovered you feel happy about an assumption that you will end up married to your estranged boyfriend/girlfriend as soon as they figures out you're the one. Their behavior, which includes contacting you sporadically and casually, with no commitment, keeps you tied up in hope. It's clear that nothing in your current relationship (or lack of one) indicates that your assumption has any seeds in reality. But it is what you want to assume, because it keeps you from dealing with your real feelings.

However, feeling hopeful about something that has no basis in your current reality is a false hope. You need to look deeper, to see where you may be avoiding or fantasizing or even distracting yourself from reality, perhaps so you don't have to feel other emotions such as disappointment—or even worse, the feeling that you deserve to be in this pain. What feeling are you avoiding by using this assumption/fairy tale, and how does it benefit you? There's always a benefit, such as avoiding anxiety, disappointment, and despair. When you have delved deeper and identified the emotions connected with your assumption, write them down.

STEP 4—UNCOVER THE BELIEF

Now, dig even deeper and reflect on the belief underlying those emotions. The belief will often be something to do with your own value, or lack thereof. It might be "I'm not good enough." In the example above, about the estranged relationship turning into a fairy-tale romance, the belief is "I am not deserving of someone showing up as a real partner. I have to settle for breadcrumbs."

Whatever belief you come to will be negative. It will not be a positive belief, because positive beliefs do not carry negative consequences every time you react to them.

When you think you've found the core negative belief, write it down and say it out loud. Use the words, "My core negative belief related to my main assumption is..."

If a corresponding feeling arises in your body, it will be clear that you've accurately identified the belief you're operating under. The physical body never lies. Every time we experience an emotional response to something, if you pay attention, you will find that the response exists in your body, too.

Once you know the belief, you have a choice. You can accept it, resist it, or challenge it. Many of us have spent a lifetime resisting, over-compensating, or distracting ourselves from our true feelings around beliefs. These strategies don't work. Growth comes from challenging your belief. You don't challenge it by becoming better, but rather by accepting it. You become better by accepting lovable, wonderful ol' screwed up you!

STEP 5—CONNECT ASSUMPTIONS, PATTERNS, AND THE BELIEF

As you can see, assumptions are the clue to your underlying beliefs (and the vicious circle of pain they create), and your patterns are just parts of the story meant to actively keep your beliefs alive. If I believe I am alone, then I will have developed patterns that will ensure I do and say things that will keep me alone. I will then create my assumptions from the results of my patterns based on my negative beliefs. It's a circle.

Now, take a look at your assumption and the belief you hold that created your story in the first place. What do you notice about the things you do and say—how do they correspond to your assumption? Look for repetition in your words and actions. How are these words and actions a pattern? How do your patterns, your assumption, and your core belief tie together? Use your journal to reflect on these questions for a few minutes, writing your thoughts down. As you explore them in writing, you'll discover patterns in yourself that you won't find by just thinking about them.

Notice all the areas of your life where you hold this belief in place with your assumption and its supporting patterns. The key is to have awareness and connect the dots all across the board. Look at the things you do at work, at home, with friends, and in your intimate relationships. What do you see? How do you feel? Sit with the feelings for each area of your life (you can do this at separate times; you do not need to do this all at once).

STEP 6—GO BACK IN TIME

If you can, follow your feelings related to your assumption and negative belief back to earlier in your life. When did these assumptions

Overcoming Insecure Attachment

start to take hold, and why? What story did it lead you to believe about yourself? If you can connect the dots by feeling it all the way back to childhood, you will develop clarity about how you have relied on this false perception, and how you have been filtering reality through it. Write down your reflections.

STEP 7—LOOK TO YOUR FUTURE

Now, I want you to answer this question: If you continue to hold the same assumptions and *allow* them to have control (regardless of whether you ignore them or acknowledge them) what will this mean for your life, in the short run and in the long term? Write down your reflections. Be specific.

STEP 8—TAKE ACTION

Now action is key. Look at your conclusions and decide what you are ready to challenge. It is pointless to struggle or overcompensate to prove that your negative beliefs are unfounded, or that your underlying assumptions are crazy. The point is to take yourself in hand and feel where you are, see how this pattern has played itself out, and then decide to do one thing that flies in the face of it. Where are you, and what action can you take?

For example, when your friend calls to say she is getting married— you allow your natural reaction. You are vulnerable and authentic. You are not trying to impress her or make it seem that you feel any other way than how you feel now. You're not concerned with her reaction, because it's not about that—it's about releasing yourself from the prison of your own making.

If your belief is that you'll always be alone, look at your actions and change them by taking one step away from being alone and toward being with people. The next time someone invites you out, instead of declining, go. Or decide to join something that feels uncomfortable, but that you are interested in. Don't do things you hate, but do things that make you uncomfortable. Uncomfortable is challenging, and the point is to challenge your assumptions by doing what you feel is impossible. It's important to do this as a challenge, not as a fight. If you fight yourself, you will become even more stuck and distracted. You will focus on the battle rather than on changing how you feel.

Write down what action you will take.

When you do take that action, make sure you feel your feelings. Do not numb yourself emotionally or take action just to take action. You want to feel its impact. You are taking action because it will give you a new experience of yourself, an experience that challenges your assumptions and negative beliefs about who you are.

CHAPTER 10

Step 7—Start Taking Responsibility

Blaming and defending deplete us of mental and physical energy. Deep shame motivates us to defend ourselves and avoid taking responsibility for our words, actions, and choices. Even when someone triggers or provokes us into reacting, it is always our stuff.

The answer is to honor your feelings and to know they matter—always. Learning to be vulnerable by transparently speaking your truth is how you honor yourself. You learn to identify and let go of the triggers you store in your emotional body. You shift from blaming others to taking responsibility for yourself. This shift culminates in experiencing true inner peace.

IT'S YOUR FAULT?

Now the fun really begins! I have given you some tips on how to change and on what to *stop* doing. Now you are about to dig into the things you absolutely need to *start* doing, if you want to be happy no matter what the hell is going on. Self-responsibility is an amazing concept, and it's even better when you put it into practice. You are responsible for every action, word, and thought you have in your life. Let that sink in, because it's true. You have an argument with someone—your motivation, your reactions, your words, all belong to you. No one made you do it. Your new vocabulary does not include the words "made me do it." I immediately stop clients whenever they use those words. It's BS.

Often people want to blame outside events, people, and things instead of taking responsibility. But this makes you a victim, switching positions on the drama triangle, which in turn depletes you. If you're depleted, how can you feel valuable? To be valued is to be fulfilled. It's about being your own best friend.

What about self-care? It isn't just about getting manicures and massages. Self-care is about healing what ails you. Self-care is taking care of yourself emotionally with your words and actions, instead of looking for someone else to do it. If you care about yourself, you have value. If you take responsibility for yourself, you have power and authority in your life, which means you have value.

Let's say you're blaming your partner for breaking up with you. They said they're done and want to be single. You did everything you could, but it wasn't enough, and they left. You were such a good partner to them in your own mind, but apparently, they couldn't handle being in a relationship.

Where is the self-responsibility in this? You *always* play a role in how relationships unfold—it takes two to tango. When you look at your part and own it, you feel better. You don't feel like you've been screwed over or blindsided, or that you had no choice. You see the reality, which means you can do things differently next time instead of repeating the same old pattern and remaining a victim.

Look at why you blame the other person—what is the relief you get by doing so? And what do you get by avoiding feeling? Take the onus of responsibility off them and put it on yourself. Acknowledge the choices you made—feel them emotionally. Do not beat yourself up; instead, recognize what you felt about yourself at the time and accept that it was the best you could do.

Blaming and defending deplete you of mental and physical energy. Shame tells you to defend and avoid responsibility. But everything you say, do, and think is your responsibility. To be responsible means that even if someone triggers or provokes you into reacting, you know it is still your stuff.

Confidence can come only from taking responsibility for your own experiences and for what you say and do. One key factor to changing the way you live is the type of actions you will be taking, and how you'll be taking them. Doing a physical action with no emotional attachment to it provides zero results. You will see the difference when you actually move yourself into becoming an expert at breaking patterns through exploring your emotions.

When you do not honor your feelings, you are treating yourself as though you don't matter. Changing yourself by honoring your feelings—taking responsibility for them—is the work. After all, if you do not honor your feelings, who will?

THE NEW GAME IN TOWN— SELF-RESPONSIBILITY

Emotionalizing wins over the intellectualizing you do to manage your life. It wins because it is about making permanent changes. You had emotional reactions that created your beliefs as a child, so the way to mess with those beliefs is through emotionally approaching the challenge of breaking the patterns that support them. Doing this will prove to be uncomfortable, if not painful. It's not that the new actions create pain. It is painful because of the pain already living inside you. Why would you want to keep storing pain, like a chipmunk storing nuts for the winter?

That's not to say there won't be painful things in your life as you change. Change comes with loss. In this instance, it is a loss you can handle. People who preferred perfect, people-pleasing, wound-up-tight ol' you may decide they're not crazy about empowered you.

Leticia, for instance, was used to people pleasing. She was the one who stayed in contact with all her friends. She reached out to plan parties, dinners, and girls-only trips. (During the gatherings themselves, she took a backseat to her friends—she was the quiet one, the one in the background.) On holidays, she sent cards. During her daily life she often found herself helping a friend with an errand or with their kids. Leticia was married with her own kids; she worked part time, and she was worn out.

As Leticia grew through our work together, it became very clear that as she became more empowered and said no more often, she also became less popular. She never heard negative talk, but she noticed that when she stopped performing, nothing much was happening. No one was picking up the slack. Leticia found she really didn't care, because she felt good. When she ran around for everyone, she felt insecure, depressed, and angry. By doing the work, she reconnected to herself. She found herself focusing on things that really lit her up. She made new friends who put as much work as she did into the relationship. She was being herself, thriving, and truly not holding back. She was so much happier.

Even if there is loss associated with changing, you will find a resilience you did not know you had. The resilience will be there because of the value you are building in yourself. Applying what you learn here daily will take you to the next level of your life—your best life yet!

YOU CHOSE IT, YOU DID IT, YOU NEED TO OWN IT

No matter whom you would like to blame for your choices, until you take responsibility for every relationship you've entered into, every job you've taken, every word you've spoken, and so on, you will miss knowing true peace. It is not about shaming yourself or beating yourself up. It is about accepting it. To accept means you must feel all the feelings around your choices, without denying or demeaning them. Each one of your feelings—from grief, shame, and regret to deep forgiving, acceptance, and love—needs to be felt. You might have been running away from some of those scary feelings for years; that was a choice you made back when you could not handle them, when you were too young to know you were even making a choice. Unfortunately, you had no idea you were cutting your experience of yourself short.

It's important to feel the full spectrum of your emotions. When you start feeling your feelings, you begin to understand how many times you can feel sad and happy at the same time without the world falling apart or you having to fix anything. You get to wake up and have full emotional experiences.

I want you to know that not dealing with my emotions is how most of the strategies and tactics I have shared in this book were born. Like me, you might have taken the approach of becoming a people pleaser, a perfectionist, a problem-solver, a detective, or a yes-man in an attempt to change your feelings from the outside. When you look at the choices you've made, accept that you made them out of the need to survive, emotionally. Keeping pain away was the choice. This resulted in your other feelings being blunted. You have to allow all of the feelings to feel the full range of any of them.

EXERCISE: Taking Responsibility for the Rough Feelings

Grab your journal and set aside about 30 minutes of time in a quiet space. We're going to examine your choices to exclude feelings. Get ready to dig into really feeling your feelings; pay attention to your physical body as you reflect on the old events that may come up as you answer the following questions.

1. Reflect on a choice you have made in the past—specifically, a choice that involved one or all of the following: disappointing others, judging a person, resenting something about someone, and/or blaming them for how you felt. Look at how you may have wanted to make a different choice, but because of how you felt, you made this choice. Accept responsibility for your feelings—they were not caused by anyone else. What do you honestly feel right now about yourself and that choice? Write it down. (You can do this exercise with different choices; but for the purpose of completing it, please do one choice at a time as you go through the following steps.)

2. Where were you in terms of your relationship with yourself at the time? (Examples: disconnected, looking outside yourself for the reason you felt the way you did, running from shame, etc.) How did you feel about yourself once you made the choice? (Examples: numb, sad, relieved, happy, etc.) Were the feelings you had before and after the event authentic, or were they reactions to people and situations outside of you?

3. If you had the choice to make now, would it be different? How?

4. Can you accept yourself for making the choice you made? You accept yourself by feeling the sensations inside of you—find the discomfort. Do not think it, feel it—stick with it—if you cry, then cry, if you feel like you want to run away, ride the feelings out. Do you feel any obstacles inside? I suggest not taking everything you did and wrapping it up into a big bundle to accept. Take one aspect of what you are feeling in your body at a time.

If you need help in understanding what it is to accept, reflect back on other choices, the ones you have already accepted. Why did you accept those? What was different about those circumstances, or about your feelings? There is always something that speaks to why it was okay for you to have chosen what you did back then. Why do you think other choices are not so easy to accept, in comparison?

The choices that are easiest to accept may come from one of two places: one is that you felt justified because of someone else's choices. This not true acceptance. It is justification. The other is that you owned your choices—you did what you did because it was the best thing for you at the time. Even if you would choose differently now, you accept that you chose to go to that college or skip it altogether, or that you broke up with the person you never should have spent time with in the first place. The point is to see where you have acceptance.

5. Look at the past choices that you regret—the ones where you feel shame, or where you cannot believe you did that! (Examples: I told my best friend to go fuck herself! I did not go to my mom's funeral. I bought that yacht!) You want to see yourself as you were back then, and accept yourself. Write down your thoughts, and feel the feelings you know are there. Accepting that you were troubled, or that the decisions you made may have been all you could do, is key.

What have you learned from doing this exercise?

You might find that some of your choices were based on a fantasy. Having made choices because you had a dream or fantasy about someone else is one of the more difficult things to accept. "I left my husband for my high school sweetheart, who lied when he said he was divorcing, too. I thought we were meant to be together!" "She seemed like the perfect partner, from her looks to how she handled my dad. I figured our fights were something others went through, even when she was so mean. Then when we got married, I thought it would get better. But it was worse!" Most fantasies are born from believing you can have something you've never had. You believe the intensity you feel means she is your soulmate. You think it means true love. Nope, it just means it's your good old lizard brain recognizing something familiar, combined with some fear of loss. Intensity is not a telltale sign that something is good. In fact, feelings have got to be intense when you've become numb to more subtle feelings. Often people react to those intense feelings as a sign to choose something that in reality is not currently functional. There is usually a "someday" belief about it when you can't let go.

MORE CHOICES!

Many of your choices were based on skewed expectations. I think we've all had the experience of expecting something great and it ended up a disaster. Our original, tightly held expectation was that the experience would be the be-all, end-all. When it wasn't, we felt burned. Now you can look back and see what motivated your expectation. Use the exercise you just completed to dig deeper.

Ask yourself what you were trying to escape. A bad situation? Maybe you moved across the country with the dream that your new location would be the answer to all your problems. At first it seemed that way, and then you settled in and found yourself with the same sorts of issues. Nothing had really changed. But you still kicked yourself in the ass for having made the choice in the first place—spending all that time, money, and energy just to end up unhappy again.

These choices all need to be accepted and owned. And to do that, you have to feel your feelings around them. "Yes, I did that. Yes, I chose this. Yes, I screwed over myself and others." Feel this stuff, do not run from it. It gets easier. It starts to feel lighter. And as it gets lighter, you get to dig deeper. Delve into what drove those choices. Understand emotionally the need you had at the time.

Then tell other people how you own these choices now. Seriously, tell people about your choices. Before, you were too full of shame to admit to it. You can do it now. *Admit to it everywhere.* The more you own what you have done, the less you care about what others do with it. Again, when sharing, do not compartmentalize or speak of yourself as a third person. Speak from your heart and say, "I made these choices!"

BREAK YOUR RULES AND TAKE EMOTIONALLY RISKY ACTION

You might have rules. You might have lots of rules. You might spend every day mired in them. "I can do this; no, I can't do that." Most of them, you probably never question; it's just the way it is for you. Many of your rules were inherited through your conditioning. *We always buy chicken breasts. Camping is bad for your health. Never tell people what you really think. Don't be so emotional.* One of the places you may struggle with rules is in your relationship. If anything, there's a stranglehold to keep everything smooth and the same.

You should question your rules, because most of them are BS. Then take it another step and break them! Breaking your rules is scary stuff—you do not know what is on the other side of a broken rule. It might be worse than what you are now living through. But if you break your lifelong rules in the name of emotional freedom and happiness, then I guarantee that even if it is an adjustment, you will feel lighter and happier in the end.

Breaking your rules and saying or doing what aligns with who you authentically are is a walk on the wild side. It's going against the status quo. It's choosing *for* yourself and what you want. If you're holding back in any way because you're afraid of upsetting the apple cart, you will stay stagnant. The rules you have for keeping the apple cart upright cause you a helluva lot of pain.

Let's say you've had some long-standing unspoken rules in your relationship with your partner. You fear if you break any of those rules, you'll lose them. But really, why would you want a relationship that is not based in authenticity? Don't forget, you have no idea what will happen, and you have no idea how other people really feel inside.

Don't stay locked into the rules because of untested assumptions. Just because you break the rules doesn't mean you will lose your partner. It does mean that you will no longer be tethering yourself to a weird form of control and manipulation by sucking it up to make others happy. Breaking the rules and empowering yourself will end resentment, anger, frustration, and victimhood. It marks a decision to become responsible for who you are and what you want. It doesn't mean you become a spewing asshole. It means you make choices and do things that feel good to you. Treating someone badly never feels good. And that someone includes you.

Here's an example of breaking a rule. Let's say your goal with dating is to find a long-term relationship, but you have a real problem with saying what you want. You leave it to the other person to set the tone—your rule is to follow along, so you don't screw up your opportunity. Especially when on a date with someone you're very attracted to, you withhold your longing for a long-term relationship but find the courage to ask *them* what they're looking for. They say they aren't looking for a relationship but would consider it if they met someone they liked enough. You still say nothing about what you want but decide you want to be that person they like enough. In an attempt to be the chosen one, you go along to get along, never saying what's true for you. Your rule is to keep your mouth shut and let this person lead; you figure you will adapt. In essence, you screw yourself because you think you'll end up with what you want, but you don't. Your fear of losing the person and being alone is keeping you from breaking the rule of speaking up and saying what you want. Maybe you keep seeing this person but it's always on their terms, and it doesn't lead to a deeper connection or a partnership. Or maybe they dump you. Either way, you're not getting what you want.

Breaking your rule would be telling this person from the beginning that you're looking for a relationship and accepting whatever comes from that. Yes, you would have to deal with your feelings of disappointment if they don't want the same thing, but sooner or later you would have to deal with those feelings anyway. It's better to do it sooner rather than later, because at that point all you're dealing with is the disappointment that it was not a match, rather than all the other feelings that accompany going against yourself and following a rule that clearly doesn't serve you.

If you don't break your rules out of fear of what is on the other side, you won't feel fulfilled inside. If your rules haven't worked up until now, why would that change, and how will you find fulfillment by following the same rules?

When you break a rule, ask yourself, "How does it feel?" You need to allow yourself to feel your way through it. Never talk yourself out of your feelings. That is just your mind trying to control the situation. You'll always feel like there's something missing if you can't break a rule and feel it.

You might feel your life has not often brought you experiences you have truly desired. Fear does that—it keeps you from experiencing life—the life you never allowed yourself to have. So, feel it, deal with it, and take a leap outside of your rules!

LOVING THE HELL OUT OF BELIEFS

One of the areas of resistance I encounter from my clients is embracing their negative beliefs about themselves. They don't want their beliefs to be true! They think I am leading them to a life of pain, corruption, and trouble, chaos, and solitude—because if all this crap they believe is true, who will want them? But if you spend all your time trying to cover up your negative beliefs or pretend they don't exist, you are wasting your time. You believe it in the first place; it's not about someone else.

I shout from the rooftops "I am wrong!" quite a bit. I have to, because I know that I cannot kick it to the curb. I am going to be wrong sometimes. Just because I do not want something to be true inside me doesn't make it go away. If anything, denying it allows it to grow in the dark, as was the case with Geoffrey

Geoffrey was in a dysfunctional yo-yo relationship that he could not let go of. They'd break up repeatedly then get back together a week later. His girlfriend would explode in anger every couple of weeks over what she felt were slights by him. She did not like how he treated her, and he kept believing that he was doing the best he could. Somewhere inside, he knew this relationship was not good for the long term, but when they would get back together, he would ask her to marry him. He feared losing her. During their breakups, he would berate himself—calling himself a loser. Why couldn't he just do what she wanted? He'd feel rejected because she would not speak to him. He also felt abandoned, because each time they split up, he was sure she was gone for good.

During his sessions, Geoffrey would share his negative beliefs with me. He would tell me that he felt he could do nothing right; he was a people pleaser who was always trying to solve problems. I asked him to stop fighting his beliefs and just accept that they existed. The deal was to get him out of his state of internal struggle. He felt tied up in knots over his own self-rejection. I asked him to just say, "Okay, I am a loser," or "I am unlovable." He resisted at first, but the truth was that this was his core belief. We can usually find some kind of evidence for our core beliefs. It's like believing the sky is blue—you look out your window and there is evidence. So why argue with it? The more you surrender to the fact that you have this belief, the less it takes over your life. You can stop trying to prove you are lovable.

Once Geoffrey accepted his belief, he realized how little power the belief had as he made different choices for himself. He stopped doing things like people pleasing or asking his girlfriend to marry him out of insecurity. The belief no longer looked outside of him for evidence that it was true, because he was not struggling with it, and so the belief had nothing to prove. He no longer tried to convince his girlfriend he was great (especially since she always told him how horrible he was). He stopped doing things unless he felt like doing them from a place of love. He no longer felt like he was held hostage by his beliefs.

Accept that you are screwed up, just like everyone else. You have beliefs that you might think are stupid. So what? The world will keep on rotating, and you will keep on breathing. It is key to love the hell out of everything you don't like in yourself. Why? Because then it stops being a problem. If I just say, "I am screwed up," it doesn't mean I am going to rob a liquor store. It means the pressure I have put on myself to be someone else stops. I give myself grace.

It doesn't work to run around saying everyone is screwed up except me. True confidence comes from being connected to yourself, feeling your feelings, and knowing it is okay to be who you are. It allows you to drop a lot of the inauthentic behaviors that wear you out. When you stop beating the hive with a stick, the bees will usually leave you alone. When you stop beating up your beliefs and start feeling the feelings connected to them, you get to have peace.

Feeling your feelings around your beliefs means letting the shame, frustration, grief, and fear rise and saying okay to them. Don't try to hide them or disconnect from them. Dig deeper—get to the root of the belief. The more you allow your beliefs to just exist without resisting them, the more you notice that even if you do something "wrong" or end up making an ass out of yourself, or any other normal human behavior, you won't cringe and go right into chiding yourself, strategizing how to fix it. You learn to let things be as they are. When you do that, you can then challenge the beliefs with emotionally risky action. By acting in the present moment with feeling, you walk toward that fear you avoid. Your belief keeps you in a state of fear, so by walking into it and through it—you shift the belief.

The cringing does stop, as does the evil self-talk. The more you do this work, the more you are at peace with being screwed up ol' lovable, wonderful you. *Everything* becomes so much easier.

BUILD TRUE CONFIDENCE AND SELF-RESPECT

Confidence has nothing to do with arrogance or being superior. It doesn't come from forcing or pretending. It comes from feeling connected and feeling good about yourself, even when you don't.

Confidence isn't about hiding your flaws or being perfect. It's about allowing yourself to be right where you are and nowhere else. This includes accepting the fear of allowing yourself to be seen as you truly are and even accepting how much you are still overdoing it. Let it all be.

Fear, as you know by now, holds you back from moving forward and changing your life. Being confident does not require fearlessness; it requires being real. Confidence is to state whatever the heck it is you want, when you want it. It's all about you. It isn't about defining the world and everyone in it. You allow others to come up with their own definitions.

I spoke my fears, first in a garbled whisper and then out loud. Now I mention them as though they are offhand comments, because I do not have the same investment as I used to in how people see me.

Being a perfectionist means you cannot be confident. You try to measure up to whatever barometer of perfection you hold yourself to. The same thing applies with people pleasing—as long as you remain a people pleaser, your confidence level depends on others. That means it is not true confidence. Steering clear of what you fear is a very fragile foundation to build confidence on, because the moment you are confronted by what you fear, your whole house of cards takes a tumble.

The same could be said of problem-solving. Perhaps you solve a problem and for a few moments you enjoy the afterglow as with great sex, but then comes the horror: another problem pops up and there you are, fighting your insecurities like the plague. Confidence is nowhere to be seen.

Lastly, assuming and personalizing demonstrate zero confidence. You can never measure up to the imaginary standards based on what you think someone else is thinking about you. It's impossible to be confident when you let what other people might think control your emotional state.

Being confident doesn't mean you have a handle on circumstances around you, it means you are comfortable in your own skin no matter what. You approve of yourself as you are today.

When you start letting go of how you need to be seen or known, it makes a huge difference in your value as a human being. The chase for approval depletes your precious life energy. To be valued because you breathe is a massive feat as an adult, but it's really just going back to how you came into this world. With this book, you are reconditioning yourself to get back to the place you started before all hell broke loose. You are undoing your negative beliefs. You are so much more than you see yourself to be.

If you want respect, then sweetheart, you gotta respect yourself. Respecting yourself allows you to grow your confidence. Remember that boundaries are not what you tell others, they're exercising the positive power of choice toward what is good for you and your well-being. Pay attention to what is happening inside of you by being connected to your feelings and loving yourself. Then you can love others.

By now you should be able to see where you enact the behaviors described in this book and can stop as many of them as you can. Not all at once, but bit by bit. Don't take this on as a project you are being graded on. That wouldn't be respectful of you, and it would mean you were striving rather than opening yourself to feel your feelings. To see yourself as you are, embrace yourself with compassion and respect.

LETTING GO WITHOUT A PARACHUTE

Once you open the door to the locked up, possibly disowned, parts of yourself you can perform miracles by reintegrating the parts under lock and key. You can unpack your baggage. For example, you might discover that you fear the loss of your current relationship because you felt overwhelmed by loss when your mom was in the hospital for a month when you were a kid. It terrified you back then, and you felt there was nowhere to go. It was as if you did not exist—that was the feeling. You developed the belief that you didn't matter and got the idea that loss was to be avoided at all costs.

You can feel it now. As you do, you can also bring it into context and reflect on how your life would have been different had you not developed the belief you did about yourself in this scenario. Take those feelings and know you can handle them now. Does it mean you leave the relationship now? Nope. It means it's time for you to see why you hold on so tightly, while at the same time trying to understand why you want to leave. It is not black and white.

By doing this work, you will learn to withstand emotionally what you thought you could not handle before. If you feel you have to make a choice about this relationship and you are not emotionally at peace, then you are not done. You need to stay put, so you can go through all the walls of pent-up emotions from the past. (I am, of course, talking about something without physical, mental, or emotional abuse. If those exist, then you need to extricate yourself immediately.)

What starts to happen as you feel all these feelings in every nook and cranny of your fearful beliefs is that things that seemed so scary before no longer are. You might still be uncomfortable, but you are not white-knuckling it through letting go. You just let go, because you realize you do not care what the outcome is anymore. You realize you are willing to do just enough and not deplete yourself. And when you know that you will no longer overexert yourself to force anything, you are getting to happiness.

It really becomes about feeling better and no longer being led around by the fearful stories you have told yourself. You'll find your brain has grown quieter; the lizard brain is taking a nap. The feelings you have inside of you are calming down and you are able to let go, inside and outside.

Allowing yourself to go back in time and connect changes the present moment. Becoming more responsible for every part of your life seems easier, too, because you no longer fear your own shadow. Breaking the patterns that hold you hostage comes from feeling all of your feelings and then taking action. Look at where you're afraid to upset things; there is an opportunity to take action. As you feel it, you will then take the next steps.

Right now, you have started to move into being an emotionally mature adult. It gets easier the more you do it, and you will find you are not in such a hurry to have everything go your way, based on old ideas of security.

NOW START TAKING RESPONSIBILITY

It's time to let go and learn to be uncomfortable as a way of living. That sounds horrible, doesn't it? You do not want to let go of things you hold tight to—like people, the illusion of security, and other things you fear losing. You might prefer to revert to an old strategy rather than actually lose anything.

Being uncomfortable does not mean you want to jump out of your skin or you never relax—quite the contrary. Being uncomfortable means being outside of your comfort zone, independent of the place your lizard brain likes to lounge. Being uncomfortable means being coura-geous and taking responsibility.

Living uncomfortably gets to be easy. To live this way is to live in the present, where reality happens, instead of in the future-based fantasy or illusion, where nothing is happening because you are not there. Being in the present moment means you are emotionally and phys-ically open to life as it is, not as you want it to be. When you can live with uncomfortable as your new norm (which is better than low-level anxiety or outright pain), then you will feel a sense of excitement, because you know life is changing.

EXERCISE: Living with the Uncomfortable

Grab your journal and set aside about 20 minutes of time in a quiet space. Throughout this book, a big part of your goal has been to feel your feelings. Now we're going to work with how to be uncomfortable. Change is not comfortable, but it is nothing to run from.

1. So how do you live with this uncomfortable feeling of the present moment?

2. What change are you afraid of right now, in your current circumstances? Write it down.

3. Find the uncomfortable feeling in your body. If it is in your head, then you are thinking, and it is not true discomfort. Go deeper. Get below your head—into your chest, your stomach, and even your throat. Where is the discomfort?

Notice if there is any resistance to feeling in your body. Do you want to run? Do you feel numb? Keep doing this until you finally feel something (go back to Chapter 3 for help with feeling your feelings). Allow yourself to feel everything you want to resist about your current circumstances. Sit down, stand up, walk, or do whatever floats your boat, and feel. As you feel, hone in on what is happening in your body. What does it feel like to you? Write it down.

PERSEVERANCE PAYS OFF!

Remember, as you become aware of trying to feel your physical sensations, it can be difficult to get there. Especially if you have been shut off from your genuine feelings. You might have sought experiences that kept you out of touch with your physical body and the sensations that came with feeling too much. Persevere. As a kid, you became overwhelmed emotionally more than once, and that led to a separation from your physical being. You stopped feeling like yourself. This loss of sensation equals a loss of the sense of self. This is how intensity became the norm—you might only be connected to the feelings that are intense.

STOP AVOIDING AND STAY STILL!

You will need to learn to tolerate the physical sensations that you have avoided—it means no getting up to sweep the floor in the middle of connecting to yourself (which, oddly enough, you may find yourself doing before you know it). When you were a kid, the physical sensations that came with your emotional wounds felt extreme, oscillating between happiness and despair. Now you must learn, through budding awareness and self-acceptance, that your feelings won't kill you. As you become more proficient at feeling, your uncomfortable physical sensations and emotions will ease.

Each time you feel into them and come back out without falling apart, you build more ease. It means you can sit when you want to run.

How often do you ignore things? Think about when your alarm goes off. You know you have to get up but ignore that thought and hit snooze. Or do you get up and resist the day? What if you have to pee—do you lie in bed trying to go back to sleep, or do you get up? What about when you're sitting on your couch and you've been distracting yourself from the plate that needs to be picked up off the coffee table. How long do you resist the urge to actually put it in the sink?

When you start paying attention to what you ignore and/or resist, you may notice how it feels physically. Not good. It creates a physical feeling inside of you. And that is not fun. But choosing to do nothing about what bothers you will create anxiety. You need to go toward what you ignore. This is uncomfortable, too—as much as ignoring causes anxiety, breaking the habit of ignoring also feels uncomfortable.

I promise you, letting yourself be uncomfortable and dealing with what you used to ignore turns into a feeling of connection. You start to really feel a flow in life as you go through the discomfort. The discomfort passes and you are in a freer, happier place emotionally. It really is like a miracle—the more you allow yourself to experience discomfort and change, the happier you get. Just watch!

CHAPTER 11

Step 8—Start Feeling Your Real Feelings

Now that you know how to move beyond your emotional triggers, you can feel your real feelings. This starts with breaking rigid rules and having true boundaries. Rules belong to other people. Boundaries, as discussed earlier, are about how we treat ourselves. If we want to be treated well by others, then we need to treat ourselves well first.

This chapter will help you move through the fear of loss and rejection, drop your emotional walls completely, and find the courage to take more and more emotional risks.

SETTING YOURSELF FREE

The experience of reconnecting to your emotions is all about you. It is about honoring yourself, stepping beyond the norm of what you have done and into treating yourself like you matter. It's not about using force or convincing anyone. It is also not about being an asshole. It is about being compassionate, kind, and open.

In theory, all of this sounds simple as a way to live. Implementing it is another story. This is why the experience of reconnecting to your emotions is important. When you are connected to yourself, it is so much easier to have relationships with other people. It is also easier to live the life you want, because by getting to know who you are, you uncover desires that you do not easily shake off or minimize just because you receive pushback from others.

I look at feeling your feelings as reconnecting wires that were cut as children. Empowerment comes from being emotionally whole. It means accepting what is fragmented and being okay with it, now.

You can dig out all the crap around your negative beliefs and, through feeling combined with action, change your life. It's not about discarding parts of yourself, it is about reintegrating all the disowned pieces, giving it all a voice. You will find, after doing this for a while, that fear is no longer the main voice, nor is the inner critic who's lived in your head. It's about really living.

How many parts of yourself did you disown when you were young? Did you laugh boisterously and hear that you needed to tone it down? Or that you just were *too* needy, whiny, happy, sad, heavy, boring, serious, cold, mean, bitchy, and so on? I asked a group of my clients to complete the statement "Fear of being too...." I was not surprised by their answers: "Growing up, I was too quiet and kept to myself, while my family is very outgoing and talkative. I learned to force myself to be falsely outgoing." Or: "My family also seemed to reward the kids who were not as self-sufficient with more praise, more care, and more attention." Or: "I talked too much. I was too hyper. Too energetic. Too emotional and dramatic. I was always told I needed to calm down. Now as an adult I've been told I'm too serious. I don't know how to have a good time and relax. Go figure!"

Notice the common denominator: they disowned that part that did not work for an authority figure in their lives. The key to being whole is to reintegrate those parts, to identify what you have been saying no to and say yes to yourself.

SPEAK YOUR TRUTH AND HANDLE YOUR EMOTIONS LIKE AN ADULT

I have mentioned speaking about your experience to others—sharing your feelings and speaking about what is true for you. To be clear, speaking your truth is not telling other people they are assholes. When you have been holding others accountable for your own actions, rather than yourself, you might find that you have a lot of pent-up opinions about them. Perhaps a lot of hurt and suffering lives within these opinions. But opinion is not truth, it is your experience. It has been your experience because of your choice. You have chosen to be right where you are. If you are in a dysfunctional relationship with another person then you have to ask yourself why you chose to be there.

The ability to speak your truth comes from the heart. To speak from the heart is to still be responsible for your words, actions, and choices. It is not to hammer away at others to get what you want. A client said to me, "What if you're the only one putting forth any effort? I am constantly speaking my truth to them. And they're not doing anything except the basics. Just enough so I stick around. But very little. Shouldn't they step up and match me?"

When I hear questions such as this one, I always bring it back to the person asking. First off, why are you putting effort into a relationship where you are not being matched? The purpose is not to berate their mate with their "truth," but to get my client to look deeper and see what motivates them to make a choice to work so hard. They must not only see why they are in this relationship, but also understand what they are trying to get by telling the other person what to do.

There is a misconception that if you put the effort into something, someone else is going to reward you. I hate to break it to you, but people get to choose what they do or don't do. It's a form of manipulation and pressure when you work your ass off, overcompensating, overdoing, people pleasing, and all the tactics that come with it, to get your way.

You cannot force anyone to comply with what you want. It doesn't work. It falls apart. You might put effort in like this because of your own insecurities.

Instead, you must come to your truth. It might be something like, "I am choosing to be in a relationship which is not really working. I haven't been looking at my part. I have only been looking at what you are doing, or not doing. I need to see how my entire focus has been on doing things to get you to do things I want you to do. It feels manipulative. To be honest, I have to dig deeper and deal with why I am in a relationship like this. When I look inside, it feels empty. I realize that I have been wanting you to fill up what I have been unwilling to fill up in myself."

From there you can take whatever action you need to take. "I am not going to deplete myself as often. It will take time, but I am going to stop overdoing and putting effort in to get you to do something." Basically, that is a truth, given from where the person stands in the moment—it is open, sincere, and totally honest. It is also emotionally mature. Adults who own their words and actions are in touch with their real feelings. They understand accountability. It makes a difference. Your whole world becomes different.

BEING VULNERABLE AS A WAY TO LIVE

Speaking truthfully about what you feel, where you are emotionally, and what your motivations are takes vulnerability. Most people find it hard to be vulnerable. In fact, vulnerability scares many people to death.

So, what is it and why is it so scary? Sometimes people think being vulnerable means you're powerless; it makes you a doormat. Or they think it's something the other person needs to do first: "Show me yours, then I'll show you mine."

But vulnerability is the core of everything. It means unfiltered authenticity—not holding back what you truly feel. Sharing it. Vulnerability feels unsafe, so you run from it like your ass is on fire. You're not really winning when you're not vulnerable. You're tearing apart your relationships across the board in your life, even when you think you're getting a leg up.

There is a *big* difference between vulnerability and oversharing. Oversharing comes from a place of feeling victimized—poor me. Oversharing is trying to get validation. It's manipulative because you want something from someone. Vulnerability is openness and honesty; there is no oversharing and no attachment to the outcome of your sharing. You share because it is true for you. "I like you"; "I am afraid to admit that I am scared"; "I don't understand, can you explain the information to me again?"

Let's say you're a woman on a date, and the guy makes a statement you disagree with. Maybe he made a disparaging remark about kids, when a family is something you value and want in your life. You say nothing because you're afraid he won't like you. You keep dating him, and he brings it up again, saying how kids ruin people's relationships. You continue to bite your tongue, but now it feels even worse. Initially you thought you could gloss over it. You didn't want to acknowledge that you have a different value system. You were afraid he would leave if you spoke your truth. But if you spoke up, maybe you would've found out that he says that on first dates because in the past, women have run when he mentioned kids. You'll never know if you don't risk saying what you believe and being vulnerable. The thing is, no matter what the outcome, if you had been vulnerable, you would've felt more empowered. You would have actually decided if *you* wanted to keep dating him.

Being vulnerable matters because you will not have a stable relationship that feels good if you don't share how you feel with someone. If your feelings are not important to you, how can they be to anyone else? When you hide how you feel, fearing you will be judged, it will feel bad because there will be an underlying current of what is left unsaid.

In a relationship, to be vulnerable is a strong position, as seen from the example of Angie.

Angie was married to Tom for 20 years. She often gave him the silent treatment when he showed up late to dinner after work. He also had a habit of showing up late to their kids' games and other activities. She felt burdened and unforgiving of him, which echoed how her mom kept score on her dad. Tom was used to experiencing silence and coldness from his wife. He didn't like it, and he blamed her for how he felt. Two people blaming each other and no one opening up and being vulnerable kept the two of them in a stalemate.

I worked with each of them individually. Over time, they both started taking responsibility for their words, actions, and feelings. This meant no more blame—total responsibility and expressing their truth. Being vulnerable became easier, and they started establishing emotional intimacy for the first time in their lives. Because of that, other aspects of the relationship changed for the better.

Fear of being vulnerable can lead to a bunch of sabotaging behaviors, like distancing, being on opposite teams, not being generous, expecting something in return, resentment, or wanting someone else to change their behavior so you feel okay. It is so much easier to just be open and vulnerable, but for many it first requires unlearning the behaviors you've used to cover up your vulnerability.

It might feel like you are taking a huge risk by being honest, especially if you feel the other person will not care or might use it against you, thinking, "I'm totally willing to be vulnerable if the other person goes first, because then I stay in control."

Operating from this stance, you're keeping things the same and hoping for change. You can have fear in one hand and hope in the other; both are equal when it comes to not being in charge of your own emotional state.

Speaking your truth is not about making sure someone else goes first or even hoping that they will accept what you say—that is not the point. The point is to express what is true for you. You are a victim to others when you try to gauge what to say and when to say it because you need their cooperation. This is what you may have done as a kid, needing to make sure that what you were feeling was okay with your parents. Many people were told it was not okay. By remaining disconnected because of earlier disapproval, you are struggling with the concept of trusting that what you have to say will be well-received.

Whether it's well-received or not won't change your feelings deep inside. It may, however, put you in a state of reaction to another person, which is not a truth. Reactions are caused by an emotional trigger that was usually stimulated from the outside—it is where you may try to match someone emotionally or answer a simple question with a harangue: "No, I don't want a damn hot dog! I hate hot dogs, why would I want anything on it—if I hate them?!" Instead of reacting, respond. To respond to another person is to consider what they are saying and what you believe works for you. It's not in reaction, and it's not just going along to get along. If you really don't like hot dogs, you don't ask for mustard and relish on yours. You say, "I'd rather have a pretzel, thanks so much."

If you were dating someone, you might not tell them you like them for fear of scaring them off. If they were the love of your life, they wouldn't go anywhere and would more than likely appreciate your honesty, even if they did not feel the same way. To allow yourself to expand in this way changes everything. Then when you realize you like someone, you can say, "I am really enjoying myself. I like you!" If you're past the age of 18, playing hard to get or being coy is not attractive. Those who respond to this holding back of information are usually avoidants themselves. They may not want depth or connection; they may just want a warm body temporarily, or even permanently. Holding back is not a way to bond. Bonding comes when you say what is true for you.

HANDLING DISAPPOINTMENT LIKE A CHAMP

There are a lot of situations people *think* they can't handle, such as:

- A breakup
- Loss of a person, loss of status, loss of money, loss of a job, etc.
- Failure
- Criticism
- Negative emotions—you're afraid you'll be swallowed up
- Being alone
- Being seen for the real you—possibly weak or not good enough

The list goes on from there. There is an overarching theme in all those statements: *disappointment*.

Instead of moving forward, your fear of disappointment keeps you stuck. The opposite of this is emotional resiliency—which is your belief that you will be able to handle whatever life throws you. It's not about avoiding disappointment; it's about going through it and knowing you'll be okay. Let this phrase sink in: *emotional resiliency*.

It's a huge turning point in emotional growth. Once you are emotionally resilient, you are able to take risks that previously held you back. It is emotional freedom. And trust me, *you want it*. Emotional resiliency and emotional availability go hand in hand.

All of your movement toward taking care of yourself and your feelings makes you far more resilient. You will find that connecting to your emotions, even a little bit, makes it so much easier to handle what life throws your way. You may not see the results immediately, but will usually see them when disappointment comes your way and you realize it is not impacting you the same way. You'll see that you are far more able to handle it, in a way that doesn't include a heavy physical feeling, depression, or rumination about "shoulda, coulda, woulda" in your life.

To have emotional resilience is to find you no longer build emotional walls against what you do not like or want. Your actions are no longer based on avoiding or trying to protect yourself from feelings or circumstances you fear. Finding that most of what you feared is nothing to fear at all sets you up to handle things well when they do not go your way.

Letting go of outcomes sets you up to not care so much if a singular thing goes your way in the scheme of your life. When you know what matters to you deeply—such as love, happiness, fun, truly experiencing life and being emotionally available to it—you find that life is not about things going your way. There is not a specific way life needs to happen. When life does life and you do you, you no longer have a death grip on avoiding or forcing the external to cooperate.

Let's say that you suspect your partner wants to break up with you. In the past you would work your ass off to convince your partner how wonderful you are. This time, when you sense your partner distancing from you, you ask yourself, "What is going on with me? How do I feel? Am I feeling connected here, and does this relationship feel functional for me?" When you honestly answer those questions, you may find you've been hiding out in how you feel, fearing there may be a loss. Now you decide to go straight toward what you fear rather than beating around the bush. You mention to your partner that you've been feeling a bit distant lately and of course ask them how they feel they have been acting. Let's say they seem like a caged animal, wanting to take flight. Perhaps they tell you they have not been happy or something like that. You just sit and listen, without cutting in with your ideas. You notice you're not nervous; you don't feel the need to steer them in what they say. You are okay. As they talk, if they aren't really being clear, you may step in and rephrase, so you can get a clear understanding: "From what it sounds like, you are not happy here. It doesn't sound like you have anything you want to give to this relationship to make it work, from what I hear. It's not what I want or like, but I am hearing that you are done. Is that true?" And let's say your partner says, "Yes."

You may feel your stomach drop to your knees, but at the same time, you will feel a sense of peace. It's disappointing, but you feel better at the same time, because you're not trying to avoid something, nor are you carrying the load of wondering what your partner wants now. It is crystal clear. This clarity allows you to deal with your feelings without all the usual distractions of tearing your partner apart or finding reasons why you shouldn't break up or any other hard work you would have done in the past. Instead you deal with your feelings, really allow yourself to feel, and start to move forward. You stay in reality and do not go into mythical fantasies of your partner changing their mind. You stay grounded right here, dealing with exactly what was said and exactly where things are at. A bit of time goes by, and you realize how good you feel. Even though you are a little sad, you really feel good.

That is emotional resiliency. It comes from taking the fear on, not trying to overreach your control, allowing life and others to do what they do while you remain crystal clear with yourself about what is happening. You realize, "This too shall pass." Miracles happen in your life when you are emotionally resilient.

I changed this in my own life. Back in the day, everyone I knew who was in a healthy relationship would say, "I love this guy, he's awesome. But if something happened, I'd still be okay." I took it as negative, like they didn't love their partner enough, because to me, a breakup felt earth-shattering. This was confusing because I saw these people as committed and happy, and I wanted to feel that someday, too. They weren't suffering through the drama that I was used to. I started to look at consistency and showing up, wondering if those played a role in emotional resiliency.

Yep, sure did!

I dug more into disappointment and where that played a role in my life. I also had to look at my scarcity issues around men. Matt, the guy I was emotionally attached to for years, was actually a tremendous teacher. He helped me work though disappointment, scarcity, and much more. I became more ballsy with Matt in speaking my truth, and each time he didn't leave (which is what I feared), I grew stronger.

I also noticed that disappointment didn't kill me—I could handle things when they didn't go the way I wanted. I decided to be consistent by reaching out when I wanted to talk to him instead of playing games. I kept showing up and being open, even when I wanted to run and regardless of how he showed up. I learned I'd be okay no matter how he acted.

Matt left for a year and then showed back up. I felt the disappointment well up because I knew I wouldn't be happy with him, but I didn't go down the rabbit hole. I spent a bit of time with him to really be clear, not make a rash decision. I decided after about a month that we just weren't a match. It was long enough for me to figure out I did not want this anymore. Those horrible feelings of disappointment that used to last days, or even weeks, lasted only a few hours. I felt a sense of openness and clarity that this wasn't someone I wanted in my life. I had become trusting of myself and was my own best friend.

AUTHENTIC TRUE LOVE OF YOURSELF

As you start being open and honest with yourself, you develop a kinship with you. You're not bullshitting yourself by lying about what is happening; instead, you're being real about the circumstances in your life. This honesty, along with feeling your feelings, are the keys to loving yourself. These keys open the door to a very real relationship, the one that sets the bar for all the relationships in your life: the one with yourself.

Loving yourself is not only about stopping behaviors that work against who you really are. It's about allowing yourself to be right where you are, without judgment. It's allowing yourself to be in the moment instead of in the future, where life has yet to happen. Without all the rules of engagement, you find all your social interactions have become easier, because you do not have the same expectations of yourself or others.

These are some of the things I have found in my own life. I no longer dread social interaction, even though I will never be a full-on extrovert. Instead, I allow whatever is going to happen around me to be, trusting myself to be as "me" as I can be in those situations. They no longer make me uptight, because I no longer work so hard to try to achieve anything that says, "You're okay, you fit in, no one will notice you are weird." I don't give a hoot if people think I am weird, and therefore it is no longer a beacon I put out there.

You will also find, in loving yourself, that you do not compromise your value by saying yes when you mean no. And when you do say it, you are very clear with yourself about what happened, not telling a story to make it okay. You deal with disappointment like that on the spot, instead of saving it for later. You do not waste your time hoping for what is dysfunctional to become functional. Your expectations are not out of this world. You deserve a better life, and that is now the one you are living. It's called having a life you love, because you love yourself. You can feel it, too.

You might be feeling like you've been a superstar. It's what you worked so hard to become. You're smart, witty, and everyone thinks you're a catch, whether you're single or in a relationship. Your friends can't understand why you aren't happy. *You* don't understand why you aren't happy, either. The problem is, you work too hard to present a false self. If you don't feel like the real you is capable of being happy, you try to be a different person, and that's who you lead with. This happens a lot with insecure attachment.

You work your ass off, trying to be this superstar—a version of yourself you think others will like. It's a constant search for validation, and validation never lasts, so you keep coming up with strategies crafted by this amazing person you created, sending you further down the rabbit hole.

You get mad at yourself on one hand, but on the other hand you wonder why you can't get what you want. You go back and forth between the real you and the false you, not even realizing you're doing it. It's hard to be happy when you're not authentic.

To love you is to stop every performance you give with the intention of gaining approval. It doesn't work, and it feels like slogging through mud to get there.

EMPOWERED FROM YOUR HEART, NOT YOUR LIZARD BRAIN

To be empowered is to truly own it all from the heart. When you are coming from your heart, it feels different. I have shown my clients that when they close their eyes and focus on their heart area, there is a connection. If they focus and feel nothing, I suggest noticing how they feel when thinking of a favorite animal, someone they love unconditionally. The feeling is usually the warmth of love, the feeling of expansion and lightness. When you feel that feeling and look at your life, you have a whole other perspective. Issues don't look so harsh and most things that weigh heavily will feel lighter. It is really being empowered from the heart.

The movement described in this book is about landing in your heart and making your choices while feeling this way. Good choices aren't made from fear; they are made from an empowered state. You are connected to your true self when you feel this way—it is a straight line of connection. When you have not worked on the obstacles, you will have a hard time getting through to that feeling. Too many questions from fear will plague you: "What if this happens?; What if that happens?; Will I get what I want?" It creates an inability to really be clear with yourself. Shifting out of the fearmongering inside is made easier by feeling into the physical sensations of happy, joyful, loving feelings.

The following exercise will help you get there.

EXERCISE: Making Choices from Your Heart

You don't need to pull out your journal for this exercise. Just follow the steps so you can tell how it feels to choose from your heart.

1. Close your eyes.

2. Focus on your rib cage.

3. As you focus, place a sense of awareness on an animal , a child, or grandparent (someone you feel lovingly toward—where there are no conditions).

4. Pay attention as you focus on your heart area with this individual in your awareness. Notice a warmth in your chest, a sense of expansion and relaxation.

5. Now as you open your eyes, stay focused on this feeling. Could you make a choice from feeling this way that might have been difficult a few minutes ago?

6. Any time you want to touch on unconditional love—do this exercise. It gets easier, and there will come a point where you will just focus on your heart and feel it.

NOW START FEELING YOUR REAL FEELINGS

After reading through everything you should stop doing, you should find it easier to feel those feelings. You might have spent time feeling your feelings of reaction. It may seem like you are stuck in a circle of feeling the same old feelings, but you are not. It's time to dig deeper.

When you sit with your feelings, whether in a reaction or focusing on tightness or pain in your body, you will notice other parts of your body, sensations that are begging to be felt. Focus on those sensations and get curious about what they are connected to. If you were dancing and someone tripped you, which resulted in you spraining your ankle, you would have an emotional reaction. That is a good time to feel from your heart. Feeling from your heart rather than blocking your heart and focusing on distress, emotional or physical, allows you to break a pattern. It is there that you can make a difference.

You can also feel the feelings, get deep enough to the seed of their beginnings, and watch the original scenario play out in your mind. I had a client who felt anxious and uptight most of the time. I had her close her eyes and feel into her feelings. She focused on the feeling in her stomach. I asked her what the feelings were telling her, and she said they made her sad; she felt alone. I said "Can you remember the first time you felt this way? What's the first thing you see?"

"It's stupid," she said.

"What do you see?"

She said that she saw her hands; she was playing with her thumbs. I asked where she was, and she said she was sitting on the porch of her sitter's house. I asked why she was sitting there, and she told me that she was waiting for the sitter to open the door. I asked if she was alone; she said no, her little brother was with her. I asked what time it was, and she said six in the morning. I asked how old she was, and she said five. Her little brother was four. She was sitting on the front porch of her sitter's place at six a.m. I asked why. She said her mom had to go to work, and she usually left them there. The sitter would not open her door until seven. My client felt alone and abandoned, not to mention that the sitter was not a fan of these kids and would do abusive things to them. My client felt she couldn't complain, because her mom worked long hours and was always tired and on edge. My client, who had been worried about losing her boyfriend, realized she was afraid of being alone. It would feel like no one cared about her, as it had when she sat on that front stoop.

I asked her if there was a way she could reframe the situation to one where she came from an empowered place for herself (no small child is normally going to grasp this—but your adult mind can). My client saw herself as sitting on the porch with her brother and decided she would pull out the crayons and paper from her backpack to draw pictures of how she felt. She had her little brother join in with her. She would then draw pictures of seeing herself being loved and happy just as she was, that she was okay. She drew pictures of being with friends. She felt love, and in this reframing of the past, she felt stronger, less sad and alone. She felt more empowered in dealing with the sitter. Instead of fearing the sitter, she started being more confident.

The whole way of seeing herself as empowered changed how she felt when she reflected back, and it empowered her going forward in her adult life. It was not a one-shot deal. It took time to have the courage to make changes, which included eventually leaving the relationship she was in. By the time she did it, she felt empowered and at peace. Feeling her feelings and being able to get to the deeply held feelings from past events and reframe them helped her.

Tips to remember as you finish this book:

- Connect with your inner voice to discover what you really want. Stop looking for clues outside.

- Being vulnerable is speaking one's truth—transparently, all the time. It is how we honor our feelings—and it's hard.

- Speak your truth (without ultimatums). You can only speak the truth in this moment. You can't speak about the future because you don't know what it will be. You *must* stay in the present.

- Speak from a place of personal responsibility for having made the choice to be where you are. Look deep and find your motivation for why you're here. That's where you speak from and act from.

- Action isn't just about talking. You also have to take positive steps forward. (Example: Years ago, when I was in a bad relationship, I wanted to take a sculpture class, but there were a lot of obstacles. It was *really* hard for me to take the class, but I eventually did it.) What positive things are you holding yourself back from? Go do them.

- Going toward the fear emotionally by taking risks without putting emotional walls up takes courage, as the fear of loss looms. If there's action with no fear, nothing will truly change.

- Emotional risk is key to changing the subconscious beliefs we hold. Changing what we normally do in a situation is uncomfortable—until it's amazing!

To wrap up, here are some quick reminders, questions, and tasks.

- When you feel stuck, look at what you're afraid to talk about or admit to. What is your fear around what you are avoiding? Is it fear of not being accepted, fear that you're stupid, fear of being abandoned, or fear of appearing weak? When you do what you always do, you know what to expect. Saying something vulnerable might make you feel like you give the other person ammunition. In reality, that is not true, instead you are courageous and honoring your own feelings. If you do not honor your feelings, who will?

- Ask what your impetus is for wanting to hide yourself. What makes you so horrible? Dig into those fears. Something in your past made you feel it wasn't safe to open up.

- Take small steps in revealing parts of yourself that you feel are unacceptable, or that you'll be judged for. Each time someone doesn't run away when you open up, you'll reflect back to yourself: "If someone else isn't judging me, why am I judging myself?" You'll start breaking down your fears and hopefully understand where they come from in the first place.

- Look at where you're afraid of loss or disappointment. Ask yourself what you believe you can't handle. Identify it.

- Take a step that's uncomfortable in the direction of what you don't think you can handle. Start looking for a job, or start speaking your truth in your relationship. Step by step, you'll see you didn't die.

- Keep doing this over and over, and you will build that resiliency.

CONCLUSION

Learn to Love the Hell Out of Your Life

Learning to love the hell out of your life is easier when you do not have so many conditions about what makes a lovable life or how it must look from the outside. If I weigh my college weight, am making seven figures a year, and own three homes, then am I finally gonna love the hell out of my life? It doesn't work that way at all. You might think these achievements will give you permission to love the hell out of your life, but the truth is, loving your life has nothing to do with the outside.

You can love the hell out of your life because you make a decision to do so. You make this decision emotionally, where you are committed to loving what is, rather than what you think is still missing. Many people strive to reach what they think will be the "arrival point" to the apex of their lives, only to find they get there and still feel like themselves. The amount of disappointment, depression, and/or frustration can be overwhelming because of the expectation that somehow things were going to be amazing, yet now that they're here, they feel like the same old, same old.

In all the work you have done since picking up this book, you should feel an inkling of a shift from the outside to the inside, getting closer to realizing that having a kick-ass life is based on how you feel, not on how it looks.

You have to make a commitment that the inside matters more than the outside, in terms of your words and actions. You can apply this in any situation. Yes, some people may not be happy about your choices, but they are your choices. Others having any influence over your decisions is something you have to be honest about. You may choose for someone else and against yourself, but you need to be honest with yourself and not make up a BS story. This work is not about remaining perfect, it is about allowing imperfection and learning to live with yourself as imperfect. It is not about getting somewhere else to feel joy; it is about allowing yourself to be good ol' screwed up, wonderful you.

I have found that the outside catches up to our inner shifts, and it does so in amazing ways. You might find yourself feeling excited, giddy like a small child, when you start shifting out of the intellectualizing and step into emotionalizing—being connected to your true self. Uncertainty will feel like anticipating an awesome surprise, because you will know deep inside that change is actually happening, and you are allowing it.

This book has covered all the ways you do not allow joy, why you don't allow it, and what you can do to feel and allow the joy into your life ASAP. It just takes a commitment to not beating yourself up about where you think you need to be. Be right here. Right here, as you are. As you grow, things will change.

SCREWED UP AND STILL MAKING CHOICES YOU LOVE

So many people strive for perfection to cover up feeling like they're screwed up. Striving for perfection is a lonely club, as you know, especially after reading about all the ways you might have chosen to torture yourself. Happy people are screwed up; sad people are screwed up; everyone is screwed up, including you. Welcome to the club. It's a big club and it has a motto: "Be happy even though you're screwed up." It includes making choices for the authentic you, from a place of happiness rather than fear.

The road to happiness is not through punishing yourself for your flaws or living up to someone else's standard of achievement. It is about the choices you make as a self-accepting human being. I make choices from there all the time. I do not make choices based on what other people may expect, because it feels too difficult. Like me, you will get to the point of being able to make choices for yourself that are easier. You will see more clearly that choices based on expectations, either self-imposed or placed by someone else, are never easy—they will exhaust you. The good news is that as making choices for yourself gets easier, the old ways will become extremely difficult to do.

As you make movement with your choices from love, another interesting thing happens: the dick in your head starts to shut up. Things on the inside will get quieter and calmer, rather than loud and obnoxious. The critical voice that was keeping you on a rollercoaster of anxiety and trying to be good enough will stop.

We all have fears and baggage from life. No one escapes unscathed, but you are going to take those fears and baggage out of the driver's seat—heck, out of the front seat. You do not have to be rid of any of it to be happy, you just need to accept that it is there. Hence you are screwed up and lovable. You do not become perfect.

No matter what your childhood was, healthy or otherwise, you can feel more confident with your choices. Pay attention to how you feel physically in your body when it comes to a choice. What do you feel? Fear? If you feel fear, are you trying to escape it or avoid the possible thing you fear? Or is it scary because you are making a choice that is in alignment with who you are? The latter is obviously where you are headed, the first is the status quo pattern—the one that wants to avoid what you fear at all costs.

The trick is to make choices *toward* what you fear, so you do not avoid. To avoid is baggage in and of itself. The less you choose to avoid, the more open you are to what life will bring you.

Whether you make a choice and it doesn't work out how you envisioned (rarely does any choice work perfectly) or someone in your life disappoints you with how you expected them to show up, making the choices from your heart will give you the emotional resiliency to allow things to be as they are.

Cutting yourself slack is key. It is not that you get lazy or sloppy, it is that you become aware of how useless it is to beat yourself up. You can try to fit yourself into what you're supposed to be in your own mind, strategizing a new way of doing it, hoping it's the answer, then failing. Or you can say, "Screw it, I'm going to own my baggage and be screwed-up old me." There is freedom in that acceptance, and it gives you a lot more energy. You feel happier because you're not so stressed and worried about what other people think.

Some tips on how to be the best version of screwed-up you:

Overcoming Insecure Attachment

1. Look at where you beat yourself up. Listen to the story you tell yourself about where you fail, suck, are a loser, etc.

2. Ask yourself if you can accept that version of yourself—if you can say yes to being the screwup your inner critic thinks you are.

3. Notice there is another part of you that will defend you. It says, "Wait, I'm not screwed up," and then lists your achievements. This leads to an internal struggle.

4. Raise the white flag and surrender. Stop fighting yourself and accept that you feel great on one hand and awful on the other. Neither defines who you are. Don't fuel either argument—trying to be amazing to impress people. Don't fight the asshole part, giving it energy.

TRUSTING YOURSELF, LIFE, AND THE UNIVERSE

Surrender is a word most people connect to giving up. It's not about giving up at all. It is about letting go of resistance that keeps you stuck in wanting things to look a specific way in your life. Surrender lets you say, "Perhaps there is another way that I have not experienced before, or perhaps this is exactly what I have been asking for in my life—it just looks different from what I expected it to."

When I was dating and decided I was really ready to meet a life partner, it took a lot of surrender for me to trust myself and trust that life would tell me where I was going. But that's exactly what life did. If I hadn't surrendered, I would still be single.

To surrender meant that I had no idea who I was dating, in terms of whether they were the one or just someone for a date or two. I stopped those questions and allowed things to unfold. I knew as I was doing it that I could trust that I was on a different journey, because it kept changing. I would be getting ready for a date and I could feel fear rise up, I could feel the desire to remain closed up nipping at my heels. I found that by stopping myself, getting back in my body, in the moment, feeling grounded and allowing things to do what they were going to do, I started to have fun.

I used to try to predict the outcome of a date just by seeing someone's dating profile. I had a story in my head. When I surrendered, I dropped tall tales, allowing things to be as they were without judging. Where I may have cut myself loose from dating someone, I hung with it. I did not stop. I allowed myself to be rejected and let things come to their natural conclusion.

Sure, I endured disappointment, but I also found that I could be relaxed. It helped me tremendously in learning to trust myself. That is where you have the sweetness of life. I met my husband soon after I started dating this way, without so much weight on every date or person. I was learning about me and knew that sooner or later, the person for me would show up. I knew I would not know who he was, either. I knew it would be a surprise. It is so much more fun to live when you surrender to the moment, when you say okay to life and to yourself, and trust.

People who are insecurely attached have trouble trusting themselves. It's often because they got negative reinforcement for making decisions as kids: punishment, neglect, loss of attention, etc. That led to looking for rules and paying attention to what other people did for clues to what they were "supposed" to do. As a result, they don't trust themselves to do the right thing. They look to someone or something for reassurance. Because they don't trust themselves, they hold onto the hell they're in rather than making different choices, because the unknown is too scary. They look for rules, second-guess themselves, avoid making decisions, doubt whether they can trust others, and punish the decisions they do make.

I hope that by reading this book you have learned how to do things differently. You have learned that even though the unknown is scary, you can still take steps in that direction. Trusting yourself leads to making better decisions, which leads to healthier relationships, better opportunities, less anxiety, and more fun. You'll stop second-guessing yourself and waiting for the other shoe to drop.

Some final tips on trusting yourself:

1. Look at what you feel you need from other people. Ask if what you need makes you trust them more and leads to less anxiety.

2. Realize that what you're looking to get from someone doesn't work. You have to take a risk.

3. Learn to speak whatever is true for you, which is hard because you have to get to the truth rather than a rule you carry around.

4. In every choice you make, you'll learn you survived. You'll build emotional resiliency this way, which is key in trusting yourself.

SO WHAT IF I MADE A MISTAKE? LET'S CELEBRATE!

Making a mistake is not the end of the world, though I guess if you press the wrong button it could be. Mistakes are part of being human, so why not celebrate them? Remember to pull yourself out of the black-and-white, analytical life of your intellect, which divides things into right versus wrong, and recognize that you actually have a choice.

You can choose to slip into your emotions and feel the essence of who you really are. From there you can understand that you can accept a mistake. You will feel better.

I used to cringe and want to curl up in a ball every time I made a mistake. It was just painful in ways that I wasn't prepared to deal with. The more I dealt with what I avoided in myself, the more able I was to slip out of the intellect and into accepting that I am human. I started celebrating my mistakes. Although it seemed silly, it was to make the point that I was at least doing something—I was living, rather than stagnating by making no choices. It mattered because I grew happier and felt good in ways that I never had in my life. I realized that as long as I was alive, any mistake that resulted from a choice that came from who I truly am was going to be okay. Nothing would be so horrible that I could not either make a new choice or just accept the choice I made, with its consequences.

I usually find the choices I make when I am in a hurry are the ones I have to work hard to accept—those are the ones where I may feel I made a mistake. When I take my time and really allow myself to feel which direction makes most sense for me, those choices don't usually end up on the slush pile of mistakes. Having fun in this life matters, and celebrating your mistakes is an awesome place to do it!

Here are a few tips on accepting and celebrating your mistakes

1. When you make a mistake and have a reaction to it, turn the focus back on yourself and ask what is actually being triggered. What is the feeling you're having? Look deeper than the action.

2. When you discover the feeling, ask how it plays out in your world. If it's a lack of worth, look at where you're acting from that

place. Your mistake affected others: they're not happy. Where do you feel that in yourself?

3. You may have a problem with the mistake because you are used to acting self-righteous when someone else makes a mistake. Accept your negative beliefs and feel where you made this error. Ask yourself, "Is this the end of the story? Are you done?" Recognize that other people make mistakes, too. When you realize we can all be flawed, you can start to feel compassion for yourself.

TRUE HAPPINESS

Interestingly enough, you might not realize how much of your life has been based on fear of happiness. I have said over and over that happiness comes from the inside. As discussed in Chapter 4, look at fear in your life and see if the fear of being happy is lodged in there, too. How many of your actions and words promote your own happiness, and how many promote creating challenges that stand in the way of your happiness?

For me it used to be way more comfortable to just keep creating challenges. I had resistance to happiness. I felt that I had to work hard, and that the button you push to get happiness was out of my reach.

Resistance is always in reaction to something, which means it's not an innate action. Let me repeat: it's not an innate action. Resistance is learned. And you know what that means? It can be unlearned. But boy, is that tough, when people are resistant to being out of resistance! I should know; I was as resistant as they come!

I talk about resistance a lot because it's such an obstacle to getting to happiness. Resistance means you have a problem with something in your reality; you're resistant to accepting what that is. The way out of it is through emotional connection and creative action; creativity in thoughts, words, and actions.

You can find resistance everywhere: in a relationship, job, politics... whatever. There's always something to make you unhappy, especially when you're looking for it. If you're constantly resisting what's going on in the world, you're fighting fire with fire. Fighting keeps you focused on fighting, so if you distract yourself with that struggle, there's no room for happiness. And that is what you may design without knowing you are doing it.

Resistance is limiting; it will keep you struggling in the same way you always do, looking for something (the thing you resist) to change. Even if it changes, all that does is offer you a new comfort zone; it does not offer happiness. You'll be stuck in a stalemate, and fear likes you there—it likes you in what you know. Remember, the unknown is scary to the lizard brain—and happiness is an unknown.

You have so many more choices when you're creative in your actions. If you don't like something, creative action will move you into a different place. It's all about you. If you don't like the way someone is running things, step in. If you don't like the direction of a relationship, decide if you want to be in it. Get creative by taking emotionally risky action in how you approach these perceived problems.

Emotional action and creative action are the same thing—they come from *inside*. It's not about strategy or mental manipulation. It comes from feelings; from what you want on a deeper level. Those are the kinds of actions that will lead you where you want to go. For example, I feel good when I put out authentic messages or when I do things that matter to me. I feel good when I am vulnerable, taking chances and not knowing the outcome. Creative in this sense doesn't mean artistic (although it can be used for art, too), it means you actually create something from an authentic place.

Taking emotionally risky action sets you free and brings you to happiness. It's scary, almost like a high dive, but once you jump off, you'll be glad you did. Maybe not immediately, but at some point, I guarantee you'll feel better.

Remember, feeling bad inside means you keep feeling bad inside. Is that good enough for you? Don't you want happiness and emotional freedom? Don't you want healthy, happy relationships? If so, you *have* to risk what you know for what could be better. To get through your fear of happiness means welcoming it by taking a risk. And risk equals action.

Here are some pointers on stepping out of the fear of happiness:

1. Become aware of what you can't accept in your life. Make a list. "I can't accept that he/she is doing X." When you can't accept what someone else is doing, you're fighting your happiness and living in fear of it through your resistance.

2. Why can't you accept them? What's so hard? What's the consequence of acceptance? Acceptance doesn't mean you're happy. It just means that you know the wall is green, and that unless you paint it, it's still green.

3. Take an emotional, creative risk: say or do something from a creative place. Get out of your comfort zone. Stop doing the minimum. Challenge yourself by putting energy into what you're avoiding. You will find that your fear of happiness is no longer, the more you risk in your life.

WELCOME TO THE NEW CLUB; IT'S MAGIC!

Yep, you're screwed up.

Welcome to the club. Woohoo!

You picked up this book because something painful was dogging you. You may have felt weighed down, even anxious. You've tried everything to bring about a perfect outcome to your situation, and nothing worked. You might have thrown your hands up, thinking, "What did I miss? I did everything I could!" Or "How did I get here?"

I ask you now: Has anything changed? Do you feel that the possibilities in your life have changed? There is magic in living the way described in this book. It is a challenge, but it's not like the challenges you used to struggle with. The challenge is to discover if you can live an emotionally whole life, being happy. And if you take that challenge, you'll find that you can live that life. Even if you do only a little bit of what is prescribed in this book, you will absolutely experience life differently. The more you follow the guidance in this book, the more alive you will feel inside and the more you will have to share with the world.

The Screwed-Up Club doesn't have rules, but it has a motto: "Become happy even though you're screwed up!" Being a member is way easier than trying to be a member of a club that wants you to be perfect. In the Screwed-Up Club, your value will never be judged by what you accomplish, because emotional transformation just feels good. Emotional transformation is the reward. You'll be seen for who you really are, the you who has been hiding out. And this is a beautiful thing, my friend!

References

Ainsworth, Mary D. "The Bowlby-Ainsworth Attachment Theory." *Behavioral and Brain Sciences* 1, no. 3 (1978): 436–38. https://doi.org/10.1017/s0140525x00075828.

Anagnostopoulos, Fotios, and Tzesiona Botse. "Exploring the Role of Neuroticism and Insecure Attachment in Health Anxiety, Safety-Seeking Behavior Engagement, and Medical Services Utilization." *SAGE Open* 6, no. 2 (2016). https://doi.org/10.1177/2158244016653641.

Arguinchona J. H., and P. Tadi. "Neuroanatomy Reticular Activating System." Updated July 31, 2020. In: *StatPearls*. Treasure Island, Florida: StatPearls Publishing, 2021. https://www.ncbi.nlm.nih.gov/books/NBK549835.

Assor, Avi, Guy Roth, and Edward L. Deci. "The Emotional Costs of Parents' Conditional Regard: A Self-Determination Theory Analysis." *Journal of Personality* 72, no. 1 (2004): 47–88. https://doi.org/10.1111/j.0022-3506.2004.00256.x.

Balint, Elisabeth M., Manuela Gander, Dan Pokorny, Alexandra Funk, Christiane Waller, and Anna Buchheim. "High Prevalence of Insecure Attachment in Patients with Primary Hypertension." *Frontiers in Psychology* 7, no. 3 (2016). https://doi.org/10.3389/fpsyg.2016.01087.

Barbuto, John E., and Story, Joana S. "Antecedents of Emotional Intelligence." *Journal of Leadership Education* 9, no. 1 (2010): 144–54. https://doi.org/10.12806/v9/i1/rf9.

Barnum, Emily L., and Kristin M. Perrone-McGovern. "Attachment, Self-Esteem and Subjective Well-Being Among Survivors of Childhood Sexual Trauma." *Journal of Mental Health Counseling* 39, no. 1 (2017): 39–55. https://doi.org/10.17744/mehc.39.1.04.

Bowlby, John. *Attachment and Loss*. London: Hogarth Press, 1969.

Breiter, Hans C., Nancy L. Etcoff, Paul J. Whalen, William A. Kennedy, Scott L. Rauch, Randy L. Buckner, Monica M. Strauss, Steven E. Hyman, and Bruce R. Rosen. "Response and Habituation of the Human Amygdala During Visual Processing of Facial Expression." *Neuron* 17, no. 5 (1996): 875–87. https://doi.org/10.1016/s0896-6273(00)80219-6.

Bridget Jones's Diary. IMDb. IMDb.com, 2001. https://www.imdb.com/title/tt0243155/.

Brom, Danny, Yaffa Stokar, Cathy Lawi, Vered Nuriel-Porat, Yuval Ziv, Karen Lerner, and Gina Ross. "Somatic Experiencing for Posttraumatic Stress Disorder: A Randomized Controlled Outcome Study." *Journal of Traumatic Stress* 30, no. 3 (2017): 304–12. https://doi.org/10.1002/jts.22189.

Buduris, Amanda Katherine. "Considering the Role of Relationship-Contingent Self-Esteem: Attachment Style, Conflict Behaviors, and Relationship Satisfaction," 2017. https://doi.org/10.31274/etd-180810-4896.

Byrow, Yulisha, Suzanne Broeren, Peter De Lissa, and Lorna Peters. "Anxiety, Attachment & Attention: The Influence of Adult Attachment Style on Attentional Biases of Anxious Individuals." *Journal of Experimental Psychopathology* 7, no. 1 (2016): 110–28. https://doi.org/10.5127/jep.046714.

Calvo, Vincenzo, Claudia D'Aquila, Diego Rocco, and Elena Carraro. "Attachment and Well-Being: Mediatory Roles of Mindfulness,

Psychological Inflexibility, and Resilience." *Current Psychology*, 2020. https://doi.org/10.1007/s12144-020-00820-2.

Cassidy, Jude, Jason D. Jones, and Phillip R. Shaver. "Contributions of Attachment Theory and Research: A Framework for Future Research, Translation, and Policy." *Development and Psychopathology* 25, no. 4, pt. 2 (2013): 1415–34. https://doi.org/10.1017/s0954579413000692.

Corcoran, Mark, and Muireann McNulty. "Examining the Role of Attachment in the Relationship between Childhood Adversity, Psychological Distress and Subjective Well-Being." *Child Abuse & Neglect 76* (2018): 297–309. https://doi.org/10.1016/j.chiabu.2017.11.012.

Devin, Hassan Fahim, Faranak Ghahramanlou, Ahmad Fooladian, and Zahra Zohoorian. "The Relationship Between Locus of Control (Internal—External) and Happiness in Pre-Elementary Teachers in Iran." *Procedia—Social and Behavioral Sciences* 46 (2012): 4169–73. https://doi.org/10.1016/j.sbspro.2012.06.220.

Dijkstra, Pieternel, Dick. P. Barelds, Sieuwke Ronner, and Arnolda P. Nauta. "Intimate Relationships of the Intellectually Gifted: Attachment Style, Conflict Style, and Relationship Satisfaction Among Members of the Mensa Society." *Marriage & Family Review* 53, no. 3 (2016): 262–80. https://doi.org/10.1080/01494929.2016.1177630.

Domínguez D., Juan F., Sreyneth A. Taing, and Pascal Molenberghs. "Why Do Some Find It Hard to Disagree? An FMRI Study." *Frontiers in Human Neuroscience* 9 (2016). https://doi.org/10.3389/fnhum.2015.00718.

Ein-Dor, Tsachi, Abira Reizer, Phillip R. Shaver, and Eyal Dotan. "Standoffish Perhaps, but Successful as Well: Evidence That Avoidant Attachment Can Be Beneficial in Professional Tennis and Computer Science." *Journal of Personality* 80, no. 3 (2012): 749–68. https://doi.org/10.1111/j.1467-6494.2011.00747.x.

Exline, Julie J., Anne L. Zell, Ellen Bratslavsky, Michelle Hamilton, and Anne Swenson. "People-Pleasing through Eating: Sociotropy Predicts Greater Eating in Response to Perceived Social Pressure." *Journal of Social and Clinical Psychology* 31, no. 2 (2012): 169–93. https://doi.org/10.1521/jscp.2012.31.2.169.

Flett, Gordon L., Andrea Greene, and Paul L. Hewitt. "Dimensions of Perfectionism and Anxiety Sensitivity." *Journal of Rational-Emotive & Cognitive-Behavior Therapy* 22, no. 1 (2004): 39–57. https://doi.org/10.1023/b:jore.0000011576.18538.8e.

Flett, Gordon L., Avi Besser, and Paul L. Hewitt. "Perfectionism and Interpersonal Orientations in Depression: An Analysis of Validation Seeking and Rejection Sensitivity in a Community Sample of Young Adults." *Psychiatry: Interpersonal and Biological Processes* 77, no. 1 (2014): 67–85. https://doi.org/10.1521/psyc.2014.77.1.67.

Folke, Carl, Stephen R. Carpenter, Brian Walker, Marten Scheffer, Terry Chapin, and Johan Rockström. "Resilience Thinking: Integrating Resilience, Adaptability and Transformability." *Ecology and Society* 15, no. 4 (2010). https://doi.org/10.5751/es-03610-150420.

Graci, Matthew E., and Robyn Fivush. "Narrative Meaning Making, Attachment, and Psychological Growth and Stress." *Journal of Social and Personal Relationships* 34, no. 4 (2016): 486–509. https://doi.org/10.1177/0265407516644066.

Grossmann, Igor, Jinkyung Na, Michael E. Varnum, Shinobu Kitayama, and Richard E. Nisbett. "A Route to Well-Being: Intelligence versus Wise Reasoning." *Journal of Experimental Psychology: General* 142, no. 3 (2013): 944–53. https://doi.org/10.1037/a0029560.

Groundhog Day. IMDb. IMDb.com, 1993. https://www.imdb.com/title/tt0107048/fullcredits.

Gudsnuk, K., and F. A. Champagne. "Epigenetic Influence of Stress and the Social Environment." *Institute for Labroratory Animal Research Journal* 53, no. 3–4 (2012): 279–88. https://doi.org/10.1093/ilar.53.3-4.279.

Hong, Yoo Rha, and Jae Sun Park. "Impact of Attachment, Temperament and Parenting on Human Development." *Korean Journal of Pediatrics* 55, no. 12 (2012): 449. https://doi.org/10.3345/kjp.2012.55.12.449.

Huelsnitz, Chloe O., Allison K. Farrell, Jeffry A. Simpson, Vladas Griskevicius, and Ohad Szepsenwol. "Attachment and Jealousy: Understanding the Dynamic Experience of Jealousy Using the Response Escalation Paradigm." *Personality and Social Psychology Bulletin* 44, no. 12 (2018): 1664–80. https://doi.org/10.1177/0146167218772530.

Huh, Myo Yeon, and Woo Kyeong Lee. "The Relationship between Attachment Instability and Mental Health: Mediating Role of Dispositional Envy." *International Journal of Emergency Mental Health and Human Resilience* 20, no. 1 (2018). https://doi.org/10.4172/1522-4821.1000391.

Hunt, Nigel, and Dee Evans. "Predicting Traumatic Stress Using Emotional Intelligence." *Behaviour Research and Therapy* 42, no. 7 (2004): 791–98. https://doi.org/10.1016/j.brat.2003.07.009.

Jaramillo, Jorge M., María I. Rendón, Lorena Muñoz, Mirjam Weis, and Gisela Trommsdorff. "Children's Self-Regulation in Cultural Contexts: The Role of Parental Socialization Theories, Goals, and Practices." *Frontiers in Psychology* 8 (2017). https://doi.org/10.3389/fpsyg.2017.00923.

Joshanloo, Mohsen. "Fear and Fragility of Happiness as Mediators of the Relationship between Insecure Attachment and Subjective Well-Being." *Personality and Individual Differences* 123 (2018): 115–18. https://doi.org/10.1016/j.paid.2017.11.016.

Karpman, Stephen B. *A Game Free Life: The Definitive Book on the Drama Triangle and the Compassion Triangle by the Originator and Author.* San Francisco: Drama Triangle Productions, 2014.

Karpman, Stephen B. "Fairy Tales and Script Drama Analysis." Download Diagrams for Drama Triangle DVDs. *Transactional Analysis Bulletin*, 2014. https://karpmandramatriangle.com/dt_article_only.html.

Kobylińska, Dorota, and Petko Kusev. "Flexible Emotion Regulation: How Situational Demands and Individual Differences Influence the Effectiveness of Regulatory Strategies." *Frontiers in Psychology* 10 (2019). https://doi .org/10.3389/fpsyg.2019.00072.

Kraiss, Jannis T., Peter M. ten Klooster, Judith T. Moskowitz, and Ernst T. Bohlmeijer. "The Relationship between Emotion Regulation and Well-Being in Patients with Mental Disorders: A Meta-Analysis." *Comprehensive Psychiatry* 102 (2020): 152189. https://doi .org/10.1016/j.comppsych.2020.152189.

LeDoux, Joseph. "The Emotional Brain, Fear, and the Amygdala." *Cellular and Molecular Neurobiology* 23, nos. 4/5 (2003). https://doi .org/10.1023/a:1025048802629.

Levine, Peter A. *In an Unspoken Voice: How the Body Releases Trauma and Restores Goodness*. Berkeley, CA: North Atlantic Books, 2010.

Li, Tianyuan, and Helene H. Fung. "How Avoidant Attachment Influences Subjective Well-Being: An Investigation about Theageandgender Differences." *Aging & Mental Health* 18, no. 1 (2013): 4–10. https://doi.org /10.1080/13607863.2013.775639.

Liu, Ying, Yi Ding, Luluzi Lu, and Xu Chen. "Attention Bias of Avoidant Individuals to Attachment Emotion Pictures." *Scientific Reports* 7, no. 1 (2017). https://doi.org/10.1038/srep41631.

Lyubomirsky, Sonja, and Susan Nolen-Hoeksema. "Effects of Self-Focused Rumination on Negative Thinking and Interpersonal Problem Solving." *Journal of Personality and Social Psychology* 69, no. 1 (1995): 176–90. https://doi.org/10.1037/0022-3514.69.1.176.

Mackintosh, Kate, Kevin Power, Matthias Schwannauer, and Stella W. Chan. "The Relationships between Self-Compassion, Attachment and Interpersonal Problems in Clinical Patients with Mixed Anxiety and Depression and Emotional Distress." *Mindfulness* 9, no. 3 (2017): 961–71. https://doi.org/10.1007/s12671-017-0835-6.

Malhorta, Richa. "Locus of Control & Well-Being Among College Students." *Indian Jounral of Behavioral Science* 8, no. 2 (June 2017): 231–36. https://www.researchgate.net/publication/309397713_LOCUS _OF_CONTROL_WELL-BEING_AMONG_COLLEGE_STUDENTS.

Malone, Johanna C., Sabrina R. Liu, George E. Vaillant, Dorene M. Rentz, and Robert J. Waldinger. "Midlife Eriksonian Psychosocial Development: Setting the Stage for Late-Life Cognitive and Emotional Health." *Developmental Psychology* 52, no. 3 (2016): 496–508. https://doi .org/10.1037/a0039875.

Matos, M, and Jose Pinto-Gouveia. "Shamed by a Parent or by Others: The Role of Attachment in Shame Memories Relation to Depression." *International Journal of Psychology and Psychological Therapy* 14, no. 2 (2014): 217–44.

Matos, Marcela, José Pinto-Gouveia, and Vânia Costa. "Understanding the Importance of Attachment in Shame Traumatic Memory Relation to Depression: The Impact of Emotion Regulation Processes." *Clinical Psychology & Psychotherapy* 20, no. 2 (2011): 149–65. https://doi .org/10.1002/cpp.786.

McCutcheon, Lynn E. "Self-Defeating Personality and Attachment Revisited." *Psychological Reports* 83, no. 7 (1998): 1153. https://doi .org/10.2466/pr0.1998.83.3f.1153.

Mikulincer, Mario, and Philip R Shaver. "Attachment and Psychopathology." *Attachment Issues in Psychopathology and Intervention*, 2003, 35–56. https://doi.org/10.4324/9781410609670-7.

Mikulincer, Mario, and Phillip R. Shaver. "The Attachment Behavioral System in Adulthood: Activation, Psychodynamics, and Interpersonal Processes." *Advances in Experimental Social Psychology*, 2003, 53–152. https://doi.org/10.1016/s0065-2601(03)01002-5.

Öztürk, Abdülkadir, and Tansu Mutlu. "The Relationship between Attachment Style, Subjective Well-Being, Happiness and Social Anxiety among University Students." *Procedia—Social and Behavioral Sciences* 9 (2010): 1772–76. https://doi.org/10.1016/j.sbspro.2010.12.398.

Pallini, Susanna, Mara Morelli, Antonio Chirumbolo, Roberto Baiocco, Fiorenzo Laghi, and Nancy Eisenberg. "Attachment and Attention Problems: A Meta-Analysis." *Clinical Psychology Review* 74 (2019): 101772. https://doi.org/10.1016/j.cpr.2019.101772.

Payne, Peter, Peter A. Levine, and Mardi A. Crane-Godreau. "Somatic Experiencing: Using Interoception and Proprioception as Core Elements of Trauma Therapy." *Frontiers in Psychology* 6 (2015). https://doi.org/10.3389/fpsyg.2015.00093.

Rao, T. S. Sathyanarayana, M. R. Asha, K. S. Jagannatha Rao, and P. Vasudevaraju. "The Biochemistry of Belief." *Indian Journal of Psychiatry* 51, no. 4 (2009): 239. https://doi.org/10.4103/0019-5545.58285.

Read, Darryl L., Gavin I. Clark, Adam J. Rock, and William L. Coventry. "Adult Attachment and Social Anxiety: The Mediating Role of Emotion Regulation Strategies." *PLOS ONE* 13, no. 12 (2018). https://doi.org/10.1371/journal.pone.0207514.

Rodriguez, Lindsey M., Angelo M. DiBello, Camilla S. Øverup, and Clayton Neighbors. "The Price of Distrust: Trust, Anxious Attachment, Jealousy, and Partner Abuse." *Partner Abuse* 6, no. 3 (2015): 298–319. https://doi.org/10.1891/1946-6560.6.3.298.

Roxo, Marcelo R., Paulo R. Franceschini, Carlos Zubaran, Fabrício D. Kleber, and Josemir W. Sander. "The Limbic System Conception and

Its Historical Evolution." *The Scientific World Journal* 11 (2011): 2427–40. https://doi.org/10.1100/2011/157150.

Ruiz, Miguel. The Four Agreements. San Rafael, CA: Amber-Allen Pub., 1997.

Salovey, Peter, and John D. Mayer. "Emotional Intelligence." *Imagination, Cognition and Personality* 9, no. 3 (1990): 185–211. https://doi .org/10.2190/dugg-p24e-52wk-6cdg.

Schumann, Karina, and Edward Orehek. "Avoidant and Defensive: Adult Attachment and Quality of Apologies," 2017. https://doi.org/10.31234/osf .io/au8g4.

Shaffer, Philip A. "Adult Attachment, Basic Psychological Needs, Shame, Depression, and Loneliness." PsycEXTRA Dataset, 2005. https://doi .org/10.1037/e526972006-001.

Shapiro, Shauna. "Mindfulness Practices for Challenging Times: Emotion Regulation, Shifting Perspective, Compassion for Empathy Distress." *Alternative and Complementary Therapies* 26, no. 3 (2020): 109–11. https://doi.org/10.1089/act.2020.29277.ssh.

Sheinbaum, Tamara, Thomas R. Kwapil, Sergi Ballespi, Merce Mitjavila, Charlotte A. Chun, Paul J. Silvia, and Neus Barrantes-Vidal. "Attachment Style Predicts Affect, Cognitive Appraisals, and Social Functioning in Daily Life." *Frontiers in Psychology* 6 (2015). https://doi.org/10.3389 /fpsyg.2015.00296.

Shen, Fei, Yanhong Liu, and Mansi Brat. "Attachment, Self-Esteem, and Psychological Distress: A Multiple-Mediator Model." *The Professional Counselor* 11, no. 2 (April 2021): 129–42. https://tpcjournal.nbcc.org /attachment-self-esteem-and-psychological-distress-a-multiple-mediator-model.

Solms, M., and K. Friston. "How and Why Consciousness Arises: Some Considerations from Physics and Physiology." *Journal of Consciousness Studies* 25, no. 5–6 (2018): 202–38. https://www.researchgate.net/

publication/338356205_How_and_why_consciousness_arises_Some_considerations_from_physics_and_physiology.

Simpson, Jeffry A., and W. Steven Rholes. "Adult Attachment, Stress, and Romantic Relationships." *Current Opinion in Psychology* 13 (2017): 19–24. https://doi.org/10.1016/j.copsyc.2016.04.006.

Solms, M., and K. Friston. "How and Why Consciousness Arises: Some Considerations from Physics and Physiology." *Journal of Consciousness Studies* 25, no. 5–6 (2018): 202–38. https://www.researchgate.net/publication/338356205_How_and_why_consciousness_arises_Some_considerations_from_physics_and_physiology.

"South Park." IMDb.com, August 13, 1997. https://www.imdb.com/title/tt0121955.

Szentágotai-Tătar, Aurora, and Andrei C. Miu. "Correction: Individual Differences in Emotion Regulation, Childhood Trauma and Proneness to Shame and Guilt in Adolescence." *PLOS ONE* 12, no. 1 (2017). https://doi.org/10.1371/journal.pone.0171151.

Thomas, Christopher, and Staci Zolkoski. "Preventing Stress among Undergraduate Learners: The Importance of Emotional Intelligence, Resilience, and Emotion Regulation." *Frontiers in Education* 5 (2020). https://doi.org/10.3389/feduc.2020.00094.

Thompson, Galilee, Andrew Wrath, Krista Trinder, and G. Camelia Adams. "The Roles of Attachment and Resilience in Perceived Stress in Medical Students." *Canadian Medical Education Journal* 9, no. 4 (2018). https://doi.org/10.36834/cmej.43204.

Tice, Dianne M., and E. J. Masicampo. "Approach and Avoidance Motivations in the Self-Concept and Self-Esteem." *Handbook of Approach and Avoidance Motivation* (2008): 505–19. https://doi.org/10.4324/9780203888148.ch30.

Tjaden, Cathelijn, Philippe Delespaul, Cornelius L. Mulder, and Arnoud Arntz. "Attachment as a Framework to Facilitate Empowerment for

People with Severe Mental Illness." *Psychology and Psychotherapy Theory Research and Practice* (2020). https://pubmed.ncbi.nlm.nih .gov/33124185.

Tolle, Eckhart. *The Power of Now: a Guide to Spiritual Enlightenment*. Vancouver: Namaste Publishing, 2004.

Vatansever, Deniz, David K. Menon, and Emmanuel A. Stamatakis. "Default Mode Contributions to Automated Information Processing." *Proceedings of the National Academy of Sciences* 114, no. 48 (2017): 12821–26. https://doi.org/10.1073/pnas.1710521114.

Venditti, Sabrina, Loredana Verdone, Anna Reale, Valerio Vetriani, Micaela Caserta, and Michele Zampieri. "Molecules of Silence: Effects of Meditation on Gene Expression and Epigenetics." *Frontiers in Psychology* 11 (2020). https://doi.org/10.3389/fpsyg.2020.01767.

Voncken, Marisol J., Corine Dijk, Peter J. de Jong, and Jeffrey Roelofs. "Not Self-Focused Attention but Negative Beliefs Affect Poor Social Performance in Social Anxiety: An Investigation of Pathways in the Social Anxiety–Social Rejection Relationship." *Behaviour Research and Therapy* 48, no. 10 (2010): 984–91. https://doi.org/10.1016/j. brat.2010.06.004.

Weinhold, Bob. "Epigenetics: The Science of Change." *Environmental Health Perspectives* 114, no. 3 (2006). https://doi.org/10.1289 /ehp.114-a160.

Acknowledgments

Thank you to my husband, David. Thanks also to my children, Brandon, Tayler, Ryan, and Whitney; my stepkids, Rikki, Mat, and Dustin; my parents, Roger and Sue; my brother Robert and his wife Elsie, and their kids Austin and Schuyler; my husband's family, especially my mother-in-law, Lou Ann, John, and his partner Paul (thanks guys for all the visioning to get here); and our dog, Wolfie! Thanks to my cousin Laura for the years of long walks and hikes talking about this game of life. Thanks also to my cousin Tori for jumping in, being supportive, and helping with the revised proposal. Thank you to my amazing editor Pat! Thanks also to my clients, my podcast audience, and anyone who read my earlier articles. After years of you asking me to write a book, I did, for all of you—thank you for being my heroes, too. I'm also grateful to my friends and supporters through thick and thin: Terri, Shelly, Gisela, Cindy, Kathleen, Lorraine, Shelley, Donna, Debbie, Marilyn, Jarrett, Molly, Yajaira, Denise, and anyone else I have not mentioned—love you and thank you! Last but not least, thank you to my team of coaches: Legan, Colleen, Rosalind, Max, Pam, Tracey, my partner Nan, and Erin, who helps in so many ways! A huge thanks to my agent Marilyn, who made this all possible!

About the Author

Tracy Crossley is a behavioral relationship expert, author, and host of the podcast *Freedom from Attachment: Living Fulfilled, Happy and in Love*. Tracy treats clients dealing with a wide range of behavioral issues such as insecure attachment, harmful belief systems, narcissistic entanglement, impostor syndrome, destructive self-talk, and more. Her work has been focused on relationships, dating, and career issues. With a background in psychology and an innate emotional intuition, and drawing from her own personal experience, Tracy helps her clients break the patterns that keep them trapped in the repetition of unhealthy singlehood, relationships, and not feeling fulfilling success, even after accomplishing major life goals. Through emotionally driven techniques, Tracy is able to zero in on clients' obstacles in order to shift their way of seeing themselves and help them drop the emotional armor to kick anxiety and pain to the curb. The work she does leads clients to self-acceptance, well-being, emotional freedom, happiness, and the ability to authentically connect with themselves and others. Tracy has a BA in neuropsychology and an MA in health psychology. She lives with her wonderful husband and dog Wolfie. She has three grown children and two step-children and loves being with family when possible.